With strategies from America's Top Certified Tax Coaches

WRITEOFFS

TO $ THE
RE$CUE!

How to save yourself from the burden of high taxes using writeoffs, loopholes, and deductions.

Foreword by Dominique Molina, CPA, CTS

Published by Certified Tax Coach™, LLC, Las Vegas, NV

Certified Tax Coach™ is a registered trademark

Printed in the United States of America.

ISBN: 978-0-9832341-8-0

This publication is designed to provide accurate and authoritative information with regard to the subject matter covered. It is sold with the understanding that the publisher is not engaged in rendering legal, accounting, or other professional advice. If legal advice or other expert assistance is required, the services of a competent professional should be sought. The opinions expressed by the authors in this book are not endorsed by Certified Tax Coach™ and are the sole responsibility of the author rendering the opinion.

This title is available at special quantity discounts for bulk purchases for sales promotions, premiums, fundraising, and educational use. Special versions or book excerpts can also be created to fit specific needs.

For more information, please write:

Certified Tax Coach™, LLC, 8885 Rio San Diego Drive Ste 237 San Diego, CA 92108

or call 1.888.582.9752

Visit us online at www.CertifiedTaxCoach.com

TABLE OF CONTENTS

DISCLAIMER

Writeoffs to the Rescue does not provide tax, legal or accounting advice. The materials provided have been prepared for informational purposes only, and are not intended to provide tax, legal or accounting advice. The materials may or may not reflect the most current legislative or regulatory requirements or the requirements of specific industries or of states. These materials are not tax advice and are not intended or written to be used, and cannot be used, for purposes of avoiding tax penalties that may be imposed on any taxpayer. Readers should consult their own tax, legal and accounting advisors before applying the laws to their particular situations or engaging in any transaction.

Foreword

DOMINIQUE MOLINA, CPA, CTS

They say money can't buy everything, that it won't solve your problems. It can't buy ultimate happiness or love. While this may be true in our personal lives, it does not hold the same weight in our businesses. More money in your business *can* enable you to experience freedom and success, and it can allow many businesses and their owners the chance to survive and thrive. So how can you keep more of your hard-earned money?

You may have heard that companies like Amazon, General Electric, and Facebook paid NO taxes in recent years despite their significant profits. Every successful business owner should be asking themselves, "how can I legally pay no taxes like that, too?".

What most business owners don't realize is that the same writeoffs and deductions used by these major companies may apply to your business as well. The cumbersome, wordy, confusing, and convoluted Internal Revenue Code contains hundreds of incentives for business owners and investors. The problem? Very little of the actual tax code exists to explain how to calculate your taxes. Instead, it provides a rough map for how to reduce your liability.

If right now you feel a bit skeptical, let me assure you, you're not alone in this! Most people believe that this law consisting of over 2 million

words exists to take your money. In fact, most of those words are there
to *reduce* the tax obligation for businesses. The incentives in the tax code
are there to promote government policy, and as such they are susceptible
to change. We've seen this in the recent past with tax breaks for businesses that created jobs through the last recession. These businesses received
tax reductions for hiring certain types of people who were previously
unemployed. In addition, laws designed to assist the U.S. in emerging
from the recession provided tax incentives for businesses that expanded
by opening new offices, spaces and locations. More recently we saw one
of the biggest government policies, the creation of universal healthcare,
facilitated almost entirely through tax law.

So how do the big guys do it? They primarily use five different tax
reduction techniques to rescue themselves from paying too much, but
most importantly, they hire a pro. Just like in the water, in order to save
yourself from drowning in your tax debt you need to let someone else
save you. When you not only know these tactics, but how to apply the
laws to your specific circumstances, you too can take advantage of these
rules to keep more of your hard-earned money in your pocket – legally! The five most common techniques include income shifting, expense
shifting, tax writeoffs, tax credits and spending strategies.

Most big businesses have their own version of a "Tax 911" to ensure
they are taking advantage of every tax break available to them. Their
rescue team includes attorneys, CPAs, EAs, and experts in advanced tax
reduction who work year-round to ensure they pay the lowest tax legally
allowed. The best part? You can do this, too. Certified Tax Coaches are
licensed tax professionals and act as your expense lifeguards – there to
save you from drowning in the tax code.

The authors of this book are all certified in proactive tax planning
and are some of the very best in elite tax rescue. They are focused on
honing their skills and working throughout the year to ensure that their
clients use every available strategy to reduce their liability. This results
in millions of dollars saved each year, returned to the business owners to
grow their businesses and wealth.

You'll find each chapter of this book includes your own personal life preservers. Unlike the floatable materials in a brightly colored ring, our life preservers focus on ways to dramatically reduce your tax, keeping more money in your pocket each year. Although it won't buy happiness, it does have the opportunity to solve many of your business woes and help ensure continued growth and profits.

I am proud to be an expert at preserving tax breaks and using this information to help rescue cash lost to overpayment of taxes. Together with the co-authors of this book, I invite you to consider the help you're getting and make sure you're able to grow your income – and keep it – with strategies like these.

To Your Success,

Dominique Molina

Dominique Molina, CPA, CTS

CHAPTER 1

Writeoffs to the Rescue: Tips for Staying Safe in a Sea of Taxes

BRAD EWERTH, CPA, CFP®, CTP

It takes a lot of hard work to build your wealth, and nothing is more frustrating than losing a large portion of your income to taxes. This is especially true when you sense that you may be missing out on opportunities to save. The tax code is extraordinarily complicated, and it is easy to drown in a sea of regulatory dos and don'ts when you try to find all available tax savings yourself.

Many taxpayers rely on accountants, financial advisors, and investment managers to provide their life preserver. Unfortunately, these professionals can lack in-depth knowledge about the intricacies of the tax code and tax planning, so they may not be able to save you from the most basic disasters. Additionally, they may only concentrate on reducing your tax liability for the current year, instead of designing both a short-term and long-term strategy.

If you want to ensure that your lifeboat will carry you through decades of tax-infested waters, trust your Certified Tax Coach for long-term solutions. These experts work with you to create a comprehensive plan that minimizes your tax burden. They don't just look at where you have been, they look at where you want to go. They use this information to develop proactive solutions for the toughest tax situations.

Over time, your income and your investments will grow. Even small reductions in your tax bill now mean more money in your pocket long-term. Investing tax savings increases your total earnings each year, and with the magic of compounding, strategic tax adjustments can have a major impact on your total wealth.

The biggest difference between traditional tax preparers and Certified Tax Coaches is their ability to understand and apply even the most obscure areas of tax code. Certified Tax Coaches take the time to get to know you, and in doing so, they develop a collection of creative tax reduction ideas that would otherwise be overlooked.

Better still, Certified Tax Coaches are skilled strategic planners, and they help you adjust your lifestyle and business so that you are better positioned for a lower tax bill. Sharing even the smallest details about your income, investments, and future plans can lead to big savings when included in a comprehensive tax minimization plan. Your Certified Tax Coach is your lifeguard when it comes to minimizing taxes and maximizing your wealth.

Review Your Strengths and Opportunities

If you have used a traditional accountant or financial advisor in the past, chances are you simply sent your tax-related documents along each year with minimal review. This is a habit you will have to break if you want to make the most of working with your Certified Tax Coach. Working together with your Certified Tax Coach will help you understand your strengths and opportunities. You can play a critical role in your tax minimization plan if you have a clear understanding of your current financial state.

Complete a thorough self-evaluation, so you can present your observations to your Certified Tax Coach during your consultation. Plan to come away from your self-evaluation with a full understanding of the following elements of your personal finances:

- Income sources
- Investments

- Assets
- Expenses
- Short-Term Financial Obligations
- Long-Term Financial Obligations

Next, repeat this exercise for your business. There are plenty of opportunities for tax savings both personally and for your business.

Once you have identified all of your income sources, classify them by type. Examples include salary, income from self-employment, capital gains, dividend income, and so on. Next, make an attempt to determine the applicable tax rate for each. As you and your Certified Tax Coach design your financial strategy, it is helpful to note whether the sources of income that seem most lucrative are still appealing once taxes are taken into consideration.

Ask Yourself Tough Questions

The success or failure of your tax savings plan depends on your honest evaluation of your circumstances. This includes your financial history, both the good and the bad, as well as the financial future you envision. Here are a few of the questions to ask yourself before you meet with a tax professional:

- Everyone makes financial mistakes. What were yours? Why did they happen, and were you able to correct them?

- From a financial perspective, what are your biggest successes? Did you achieve them through strategy or were you simply in the right place at the right time?

- What do you want to accomplish in the next year? The next five years? Your short-term financial goals are important for creating a plan.

- What long-term financial goals do you have? Are you expecting to fund college expenses for your children? What do you want your retirement to look like? Finding ways to link your short-term and long-term goals is a critical part of your comprehensive financial plan.

- How do you define financial success? At what point will you feel that you have accomplished your goals?
- Take stock of your lifestyle. Are you willing to change how you live if necessary now to achieve future financial success?
- Consider your ability to tolerate risk. How do you feel about uncertainty, and even potential loss, in exchange for the possibility of larger rewards?
- Think about your perspective on taxes. Are you willing to take an aggressive approach to drive your tax rates down, or are you more comfortable staying away from anything an auditor might question?
- Do you have any serious medical conditions for which you require care? How will you pay for healthcare and manage your finances if you develop an illness or become disabled in the future?

A lot goes into creating your financial strategy, and all of these factors contribute to achieving your goals. Since financial success looks different for everyone, a one-size-fits-all approach is simply not effective. Sharing your honest responses to these tough questions with your Certified Tax Coach increases the likelihood of developing a customized tax reduction strategy that works.

Examine External Factors

Your skills, preferences, and financial goals aren't the only factors in your success. There are a variety of external elements that dramatically impact your ability to build wealth. Economic cycles and the political landscape are two influential issues to consider. For example, the 2017 passage of the Tax Cuts and Jobs Act completely transformed the country's approach to taxation.

Here are issues to consider when creating your financial strategy, especially if you own a business:

- What marketplace trends have potential to impact your business in the short-term, both positively and negatively?

- What marketplace trends have potential to impact your business in the long-term, both positively and negatively?

- Have you noticed any trends in value-based equity? Is there a pattern to the increases and decreases?

- Consider some of the market scenarios that could play out. What would your cash flow needs be for each?

- How will you know that you are on track to meet your financial goals? What benchmarks can you set to monitor your progress?

- What risks are likely to impact your financial plan? Inflation, devaluation of currency, reduced value of passive investments, major market changes, and significant life events can all take you off course.

Although it isn't possible to predict the future with 100 percent certainty, you are sure to be more successful when your predictions are based on deep understanding of market conditions. Take the time with your Certified Tax Coach to examine factors outside of your control; this will help you mitigate risks that might affect your financial future with appropriate action, thoughtful diversification, and relevant insurance protection.

Consider Your Capital Gains

When you choose the right investments, you have the excitement of watching your portfolio's value grow. It feels like there is no downside, until that increased value drives your tax bill up, significantly reducing your total earnings.

The difference between what you paid for your assets and their value at liquidation is referred to as capital gains, and the related taxes can be substantial. Fortunately, with planning, you can reduce your tax bill significantly.

These are some common strategies for keeping capital gains taxes low:

- Timing is everything when it comes to buying and selling your assets, and it is particularly important when it comes to taxation of capital gains. By selling high-value assets in years when your tax bracket is lower, you can minimize your tax expense.

- Your investment losses may offset capital gains when both appear on your tax returns in the same year. Depending on the circumstances, you may be able to offset up to $3,000 in regular income. If you have additional losses, you may be able to carry a portion over to the next year to offset other gains.

- Many taxpayers make generous contributions to their favorite non-profits each year. If you plan ahead, you can enhance your tax savings at the same time. Instead of writing a check, simply gift appreciated stock to the charity of your choice. You can deduct the full value of the stock on your return, but because you haven't liquidated your assets, you don't realize capital gains. That means you won't incur capital gains taxes.

- Even those who never invest in equities are likely to incur capital gains taxes if they don't take care when buying and selling real estate. Fortunately, with the right strategy, you may be able to avoid this tax expense. If you purchase a property and use it as your primary residence, the first $250,000 in capital gains is exempt from taxation. This figure doubles to $500,000 for couples who are married. You just need to live in the residence 2 out of the last 5 years.

- There are a variety of incentives designed to encourage retirement savings, and reduction in tax liability is high on the list of available benefits. Fund a traditional IRA or 401(k) with pre-tax dollars and delay your tax bill until you eventually leave the workforce. Contribute to a Roth IRA with after-tax income, and watch your wealth grow completely tax-free.

- The cost of healthcare is growing exponentially, and there is no indication that this trend will change any time soon. Setting funds aside in a Health Savings Account ensures you have cash available to manage co-payments and co-insurance as necessary.

Better still, contributions to an HSA are not taxed, and neither are your earnings. Just keep in mind that there is an annual contribution limit.

- When you sell an asset, you have some choices. You can either take the cash and use it as you please, you can reinvest it in another class of assets, or you can reinvest it in a similar type of asset. If you have realized significant capital gains, you can eliminate the capital gains taxes altogether with a 1031 exchange. This tax minimization technique works when you reinvest the proceeds from your sale of assets into another, similar investment. The transaction must be complete within 180 days of your initial sale to qualify for these savings.

- Some of the wealth you have accumulated may be intended for your beneficiaries after your death. If this is the case, you may wish to skip the sale and transfer the asset intact. Upon inheriting the asset, your beneficiaries are probably not going to be liable for capital gains taxes, as their cost basis will match the asset's current value at the time ownership is transferred.

- Your loved ones may be in a lower tax bracket than you are, which means gifting an asset could be more valuable than gifting cash. Although selling the investment might not lead to substantial gains for you once taxes are paid, the calculation is quite different when lower tax rates are applied. When you gift appreciated investments, your cost basis goes with them, but your tax rate doesn't.

Capital gains taxes create a frustrating paradox. The more an investment increases in value, the more you lose to the IRS. Careful application of tax minimization strategies can ensure that you benefit from more of those gains.

Protecting Your Wealth Through Trusts

When dangerous tax conditions threaten your wealth building strategy, trusts can be the ultimate lifeboat. They are specifically designed to protect the value of your estate for your beneficiaries. Through the power of trusts, you can reduce the estate taxes your beneficiaries must pay, and you can minimize the complication and expense of probate. Trusts make it possible to transfer wealth without court costs and attorney's fees, so more of the wealth you earned over your lifetime goes to your loved ones.

Essentially, trusts are a safe repository for your assets, and they serve to ensure your wealth is protected for your beneficiaries. Each can be customized based on the individual needs of your beneficiaries, and you can ensure that funds are used according to your wishes.

Many trusts are designed so that you maintain control over the included assets until your death. Once you pass away, funds are distributed according to your explicit instructions. This is particularly helpful if you plan to provide financial support for a loved one who is unable to effectively manage money. When they lack the motivation or the ability to spend wisely, you can create a trust that guards against waste.

You can choose when assets held in trust are released. For example, your beneficiaries may receive assets when they reach a certain age or achieve a milestone. More important, you can specify circumstances under which funds will not be released, and if you are concerned about irresponsible spending, you can set the rate at which assets are distributed to beneficiaries.

Trusts for the purpose of transferring wealth to surviving spouses and children are popular, closely followed by skip-generation trusts that provide for grandchildren. These programs give you an opportunity to care for your loved ones, even when you are no longer around.

There are certain terms that you will hear often relating to trusts:

- **An "A" Trust** – This refers to a trust specifically intended to provide for your spouse. It transfers assets immediately, avoiding the delays and expenses of probate.

- **A "B" Trust** – Unlike the A Trust, a B Trust is intended to completely bypass a surviving spouse's estate. This ensures that your spouse does not incur estate tax liability.

- **Irrevocable Trust** – Transferring assets to an irrevocable trust is a permanent decision. Once the trust owns the assets, they belong to the beneficiaries of the trust. The upside is that you are no longer responsible for any taxes on these assets. This makes irrevocable trusts a popular choice for housing assets that are increasing in value at a rapid rate.

- **Revocable Trust** – If you choose a revocable trust, you can put assets in and take them out as you please. However, this flexibility comes with tax ramifications, and you will likely pay more in taxes than you would with an irrevocable trust.

Insurance: The Ultimate Life Preserver

The benefits of life insurance extend far beyond providing extra security for your family if you pass away unexpectedly. These products can play an important role in your wealth building strategy. Unfortunately, many people simply take the standard term policies offered through their employers, without exploring the many additional options available.

Term life policies are designed to replace a portion of your income when you die. They are a popular choice for life insurance products, because premiums are relatively low. You purchase a policy to cover yourself for a set period of time, for example 10 years, and you make regular payments to keep the policy in force.

Term life is a standard component of financial planning when you are responsible for supporting dependents in the early years of your career. For example, parents with young children leverage term life to ensure that if disaster strikes, their little ones won't go without. You can choose a policy large enough to pay off major debts. For example, many people choose a policy that will pay off their mortgage, so their surviving spouse can afford to stay in the family home.

The downside of a term life policy is that it doesn't build any lasting value. It works the same way of renting vs buying. At the end of the term, it is as if the policy never existed at all. For income replacement, a term policy is the way to go, but if you want to build wealth, consider additional life insurance products.

Permanent life insurance policies combine the best features of term life insurance with wealth-building investments to create an entirely different opportunity. You still pay regular premiums, and the policy's benefits are paid to your family if you pass away. The difference is that unlike term life insurance, permanent life insurance policies build cash value. You can borrow against the policy if you face a cash crunch, as well as provide additional tax-free income if designed properly. Additionally, you can fund a life insurance trust with a permanent life insurance policy.

If you choose a life insurance trust, you simplify the process of transferring assets to your beneficiaries. Your loved ones have fast, easy access to the funds they need to stay up-to-date on bills, pay estate taxes, and cover business expenses. The best way to keep taxes low on this type of trust is to make the trust irrevocable. Lower estate taxes rates apply, and assets are transferred to your beneficiaries without the time and expense of going through the probate process.

Leverage Tax-Advantaged Retirement Programs

Every election cycle puts Social Security in the spotlight, which indicates that the program could change before your turn comes to draw benefits. Creating your own retirement savings plan is more critical than ever before. Fortunately, lawmakers have designed a variety of tax-advantaged products that make it easier to set money aside. With these products you can grow your savings quickly, thanks to deferred taxes or tax-free earnings.

The most popular retirement programs are designed to defer tax liability. Examples include the traditional Individual Retirement Account (IRA) and the 401(k). Contributions are made with pre-tax dollars, and you don't pay taxes until you withdraw funds. The alternative is a product like the Roth IRA, which permits you to contribute with after-tax funds. The benefit is that earnings grow tax-free, so you have no tax liability when you take distributions.

With either type of account, you should consult your Certified Tax Coach before pulling any money out. There are requirements you must meet to retain the tax advantages, and a single misstep can erase any tax savings. As a general rule, it is best to take distributions from a tax-deferred account when your income falls into your lowest tax bracket. Keep in mind that you don't want to take a distribution so large that it will push you into paying a higher tax rate.

If a withdrawal from your tax-deferred account threatens to cost you too much in taxes, you may be better off taking a distribution from your Roth IRA instead. You have already paid taxes on the contributions you made, and your earnings are completely tax-free. As a result, you won't owe taxes on withdrawals from these accounts. Having a strategic plan is more important than ever.

The Importance of Estate Planning

The final consideration in a comprehensive tax minimization plan is transferring your wealth to your beneficiaries after you die. You put decades of hard work into building your estate, and you don't want to lose large amounts to the IRS. There was a time when estate tax rates were nearly 50 percent of an estate's total value. While this is no longer the case, you should consider that tax laws could change again by the time they are applied to your situation.

As a result of the American Taxpayer Relief Act of 2012, up to $5.43 million of your estate could be transferred tax-free. That figure has nearly doubled as a result of the 2017 Tax Cuts and Jobs Act (TCJA). The combined estate and gift tax rate is currently 40 percent. With the right strategies, you can minimize other expenses, such as capital gains taxes, to virtually eliminate tax liability for your beneficiaries.

Maximize Savings and Minimize Taxes

Your circumstances are constantly changing, and so are tax laws, so tax minimization strategies that worked last year may not be as effective this year. Your Certified Tax Coach can ensure that your plans are adjusted to account for your major life events, as well as any adjustments to the tax code.

Take a proactive approach to tax minimization by reviewing your strategy with a professional regularly. As your lifestyle, financial goals, and tolerance for risk change, make sure that your wealth building and tax minimization plans do, too. Flexibility and adaptability are important characteristics for long-term success when it comes to staying afloat in a sea of taxes.

ABOUT THE AUTHOR

Brad Ewerth, CPA, CFP®, CTP

Brad Ewerth, C.P.A., CERTIFIED FINAN-CIAL PLANNER™ is the President and Founder of Ewerth & Associates, C.P.A., P.C. and P23 Financial, Inc. in Lincoln, NE.

Brad has been helping professionals with tax and retirement planning in numerous states for over 30 years. He has a unique way of coordinating the retirement and tax planning process, helping to minimize the impact of taxes. Recently he achieved the Certified Tax Planner designation from the American Institute of Certified Tax Planners, Inc. recognizing him as a Tax Reduction Specialist.

Due to his commitment to helping professionals with financial planning, Brad has also achieved the designation of CERTIFIED FINANCIAL PLANNER™. Less than 20% of practicing financial advisors in the industry can claim this distinction, and Brad is one who also has tax planning expertise. Brad enjoys making a difference in the lives of business owners and shows his passion for long-term, meaningful professional relationships with his clients.

Brad is a lifelong learner who continues to participate in various conferences and self-study courses. This allows him to provide leading edge tax reduction and retirement planning concepts to his clients.

Active in his community, Brad has coordinated the Alpha program at St. Marks United Methodist Church, volunteered at the People's City Mission and Center for People in Need, and is a supporter of Fellowship of Christian Athletes and Make-A-Wish foundation.

Brad Ewerth, CPA, CFP®, CTP

Ewerth & Associates, C.P.A., P.C.

📞 402-486-3777

📍 237 So. 70th Suite 219, Lincoln, NE 68510

🌐 www.VIPmoneyresults.com

✉ brad@ewerthcpa.com

Staying Afloat: How Your Business Structure Impacts Your Tax Liability

DAVID AUER, CPA, MS, PFS, CGMA, JD, LLM IN TAXATION, CTC

Some small companies begin as side projects that gradually evolve into substantial income producing businesses. Others make their first sale on their grand opening day, after entrepreneurs have put months of careful planning into the business launch. In both cases, it is easy to get caught up in the critical details of developing a supply chain, marketing products, and arranging for distribution. Other decisions, such as how the business should be structured, might be set aside for later.

Unfortunately, for some companies, a delay is life-threatening. They are swept away in a riptide of taxes. However, there is still hope. A Certified Tax Coach is standing by, prepared to throw a life preserver. These highly qualified professionals have deep expertise in how the selection of a business entity impacts tax liability long-term. They can help you choose the best structure for your business at any point in the company's life cycle, so that you can keep taxes low and profits high.

The Benefits of Owning Your Own Business

Every financial decision you make comes with risk. The more you are willing to risk, the greater your potential reward. This is particularly true when it comes to owning a business. Many people choose to work for others because they want the security of a regular paycheck. However, few are able to accumulate significant wealth this way. A majority of people who are financially successful owe their success to launching a business of their own.

The benefits of starting a company go beyond the satisfaction of bringing an idea to life and being your own boss. You also enjoy more control over how finances are managed, as well as greater access to any profits generated. Better still, both you and your organization can take advantage of a wide range of tax incentives specifically designed to encourage business growth.

As an employee, you have two basic options for building wealth. You can chase after more lucrative positions to increase your earnings, or you can spend less. As a business owner, these options are still fundamental to your success, but there are endless possibilities when it comes to options for growing revenues and reducing expenses. If you aren't satisfied with your current profits, there are opportunities for a change in strategy, a business expansion, or implementation of new efficiencies. Better still, the tax regulations for business income are typically more favorable than the regulations for individuals, so you can partner with your Certified Tax Coach to bring tax liability to a bare minimum.

Preventing a Tax Tsunami through Careful Selection of Your Business Entity

If you aren't seeing lower taxes that usually come with owning a business, you might be operating under the wrong business structure. Making a bad choice here, or no choice at all, can subject you to paying taxes twice on the same income. Selecting the most appropriate business entity can be a complicated undertaking. Related tax regulations are highly complex, and small nuances in the tax code can make a big difference to your bottom line. Fortunately, your Certified Tax Coach is ready to rescue you from the tax tsunami with advice and guidance on making the best possible choice for your situation.

The business entity you select is essentially the foundation upon which you build the organization. It legally defines the structure of your business and affects how you are taxed, your personal liability for company related debt, and whether you can be held personally accountable for legal claims against the business. For example, under some business entities, you and the company are considered a single individual for tax and legal purposes. With other options, you and the company are completely separate parties. There are even in-between options that give you some flexibility. Begin the process by asking yourself the following questions:

How much time and money can you invest in setting up your business structure?

Certain business entities require little or no paperwork, and they cost almost nothing to get started. This type of structure makes sense for entrepreneurs opening a microbusiness or testing out a side gig. However, if you are launching a company that you plan to grow quickly, another option may be a better choice. Investing time and money into structuring your business now can save you a lot of headaches in the future.

How will your business be financed?

When you and your business are the same legal entity, your company's ability to get credit depends on your own creditworthiness. You can be held personally responsible for the debts of your business. That may not be a problem, particularly if you are operating with minimal debt, but organizations that rely on financing should be wary. If something goes wrong, everything you have worked for can be swept away in a flood of creditors. There are business entities that exist separately from you, and you can't be held personally accountable if the company goes under. This benefit is intended to encourage innovators to explore opportunities and take risks to fill unmet consumer needs.

How much personal liability are you willing to risk?

The entities that separate responsibility for personal and business debt offer the same benefit for legal liability. If you choose one of these business entities, you are unlikely to face liability if your business is sued.

This is a critical consideration in high-risk industries, particularly if you have substantial personal wealth.

How do you plan to leave your business?

Few entrepreneurs are interested in discussing their eventual departure from the company when their attention is focused on getting the doors open. However, the business entity you choose now may limit your long-term options. When you and your business are one and the same for legal and tax purposes, the company lives and dies with you. On the other hand, when you are separate entities, the business continues to operate if you move on to other ventures. Entrepreneurs with a long-term strategy that includes selling the company must consider how the organizational structure will impact their future options.

Have you considered how your income will be taxed under each business entity?

The final consideration in structuring your business is the tax implications of each option. Your bottom line depends on minimizing tax expense, but there is no one-size-fits-all approach. Your Certified Tax Coach has the experience and expertise you need to determine which business entity will keep your tax liability low.

Business Entity Basics

Once you have worked your way through the preliminary questions, the next step is to examine your options in greater detail. Compare the pros and cons of each business entity to your list of must-haves, so you can narrow down your choices. If you are still unsure after going through this guide, don't worry. Your Certified Tax Coach is standing ready to throw you a life preserver.

Sole Proprietorships

If you jumped into a startup business without worrying about paperwork, don't worry. There is an automatic life boat waiting for you. By default, your small business is considered a sole proprietorship. You are operating under your own name and tax identification number, and any income you earn through your company is taxed when you file your personal tax returns.

The downside to this method of taxation is that you may pay taxes twice on the same income. You could be responsible for both standard income tax and self-employment tax. It is also worth noting that individuals operating sole proprietorships face IRS audits more frequently than other business entities. Your Certified Tax Coach can provide important information on minimizing this risk.

Operating your sole proprietorship under a business name other than your own requires a few extra steps, but the default sole proprietorship business entity still applies. The only additional action you must take is to register your business with the appropriate government agency. On legal documents, such as bank accounts, you will be known as "Your Name" DBA (doing business as) "Company Name." Of course, if the products or services you provide are regulated and require permits, licenses, or certifications, you are still required to comply.

Limited paperwork and low fees aren't the only benefits of being a sole proprietor. You can hire employees while still retaining full control of the company you founded. All profits are yours to distribute, keep, or reinvest as you see fit. If you leave the business, it no longer exists in its current form, but you can sell the assets you have accumulated to a new owner, who is free to operate under the same business name.

It can be tempting to stick with this default business entity after you learn how simple it is to launch a sole proprietorship; however, there are important risks to consider. You have complete control over your company, and all of the profits belong to you. However, you are also personally responsible for all liabilities. As a sole proprietor, you and your company are the same entity for legal and financial purposes, so creditors can collect business debts from your personal assets. If your company is sued and you lose your case, judgments can be assessed against you personally. Conversely, if you are sued as an individual, your business assets may be included in any judgments against you.

Some of the real-life situations that have decimated sole proprietors include the following:

- An employee was injured in the course of performing his job. He alleged that the injury was due to negligence by his employer. Because his employer was a sole proprietor, he named both the business and the business owner in his lawsuit. He was awarded damages that exceeded what the business could pay, and some of his employer's personal assets had to be liquidated and turned over to satisfy the debt.

- A sole proprietor was involved in a car accident unrelated to the business, and it was later determined that she caused the crash. Another person was injured, and a civil suit was filed. When the victim was awarded damages for her injuries, the sole proprietor didn't have enough personal assets to cover the debt. Her business assets were pulled into the case, and the company was quickly bankrupted.

- In an attempt to increase production and grow the company, a small business took out a large line of credit. Unfortunately, the expected increase in revenue never came, and the business could not repay the amount borrowed. Eventually, the business went bankrupt, and assets were sold to settle these and other debts. However, it simply wasn't enough to cover the entire outstanding credit line balance. Because the business was set up as a sole proprietorship, the financial institution that granted the loan was able to collect from the owner's personal assets.

Without a clear line between personal and business liability, owners of sole proprietorships open themselves up to personal risk. Your Certified Tax Coach is an excellent resource for calculating the tax impact of choosing a sole proprietorship as your business entity, and an attorney specializing in business law will help you weigh the pros and cons when it comes to liability.

Advantages of Sole Proprietorships

- Minimal paperwork required for launch
- Low start-up and administration fees
- Nominal ongoing expense

Disadvantages of Sole Proprietorships

- Limited protection from liability
- Potential to be taxed twice on the same funds (income tax and self-employment tax)
- Greater risk of being selected for an IRS audit

Partnerships

There is safety in numbers, and many small businesses are successful because they benefit from the creativity and innovation of two or more owners. While these business entities share many of the same risks and rewards that sole proprietorships face, the fact that there is more than one owner puts the company in a different category. This business structure is referred to as a partnership, and there are a few additional caveats to keep in mind before committing.

For tax and legal purposes, partnerships are the default business entity if company owners take no action to create an alternative structure. This applies whether or not a formal partnership agreement is created. This creates an interesting dynamic when one partner decides to leave the business. Partnerships aren't fluid, so when any of the founding partners move on, the company is essentially dissolved. Of course, it can be quickly recreated, either as a sole proprietorship or a partnership with the remaining owners, but it is technically a brand-new organization.

Partnerships are taxed in the same manner as sole proprietorships, which means you face the possibility of being taxed twice on the same income. The business is considered a pass-through entity, and profits are divided between the partners according to their partnership agreement. When each individual files personal tax returns, profits from the business may be subject to regular income tax as well as self-employment tax.

Partnerships face the same legal liabilities as sole proprietorships, but there is an additional risk to consider. Not only are you personally responsible for business liabilities, but you may also find yourself taking personal financial responsibility for the actions of your partner. This point, above all others, is the most important reason to work with your legal advisors on drafting and executing a formal partnership agreement. You can't eliminate this risk, but you can minimize it.

Advantages of Partnerships

- Minimal paperwork required for launch
- Low start-up and administration fees
- Nominal ongoing expense
- Shared responsibility for debts incurred by the business

Disadvantages of Partnerships

- Potential for strategic differences between partners
- Possibility of being held responsible for the actions and debts of partners
- Limited protection from liability
- Potential to be taxed twice on the same funds (income tax and self-employment tax)
- Greater risk of being selected for an IRS audit

Corporations

Industry leaders commonly choose to incorporate, but that doesn't mean this option is only available to massive organizations. Many small and medium-sized businesses also structure their companies as corporations. The primary benefit of this business entity is the separation of personal and professional affairs.

Corporations are distinct from their owners for legal and tax purposes. They have unique tax identification numbers, and there is a separate set of tax returns filed each year. Profits are considered income for the business itself, and corporations are exclusively accountable for the debts they incur. Owners receive a portion of the profits based on shareholder agreements if there are multiple shareholders, or all of the profits if they are the single shareholder. However, this amount is treated as dividends instead of regular or self-employment income. Certain tax obligations still apply, but the burden of being taxed twice on the same income is lifted.

Corporations enjoy a sort of immortality, because their existence is not dependent on a single person. When founders, owners, and managers move on to other opportunities, the corporation remains intact. This is true whether the corporation is privately held by one individual or many, and it doesn't change if a decision is made to offer ownership shares for sale to the public.

Whether corporations are privately held or publicly traded, owners cannot be held personally accountable for the company's liabilities. The business takes full responsibility for the debts it incurs, and owners need not worry about risking their personal wealth if the corporation becomes the target of a lawsuit.

With all of these benefits, many entrepreneurs wonder why anyone would choose a sole proprietorship or partnership. The most common reason that small businesses don't incorporate is the complexity of the process. Setting up a corporation is labor-intensive, and you can expect plenty of paperwork. Related fees and ongoing expenses can be costly, which is a disadvantage for small companies. Fortunately, lawmakers have taken steps to encourage small business growth by creating a variety of business entities that fall under the corporation umbrella. Under certain circumstances, even the smallest of small businesses can enjoy the benefits of incorporating without excessive startup and administrative fees. Some of your options include:

C-Corporations

The colossal businesses you think of when you picture a corporation are nearly all structured as C-Corporations. This is the traditional method of incorporating, because it offers maximum flexibility in terms of encouraging investment and growth. Under the C-Corporation entity, there are no limits to the number of shareholders. More important, other businesses can purchase stock in C-Corporations, which increases the company's ability to raise capital.

For legal and tax purposes, C-Corporations are their own entity, and they are solely responsible for all revenues and debts. A tax return is filed using the tax ID assigned to the corporation, and the C-Corp can take advantage of the many deductions and credits exclusively available to corporations. Shareholders—even if one person owns 100 percent of the company's shares—pay taxes on dividend income received from the business. They are not responsible for standard income taxes, self-employment taxes, and similar.

Business owners who take an active role in managing the corporation typically arrange for the business to pay them a salary. For tax purposes, this amount is treated as any other earned income, and business owners are bound by the same regulations as other employees.

Setting up a C-Corporation is a significant undertaking, and it is unusual for small businesses to choose this path. In most cases, your advisors and your Certified Tax Coach will guide you toward another type of corporation unless your strategic plan includes offering shares for purchase by the general public.

Advantages of C-Corporations

- No limit to the number of owners and shareholders
- Separation between business and business owner for legal and financial purposes
- Access to tax deductions and credits reserved for corporations
- 21 percent flat tax rate (25 percent for personal service corporations)

Disadvantages of C-Corporations

- Significant complexity and cost associated with start-up
- Ongoing expenses related to administration
- Owners are taxed on any dividends received

S-Corporations

Organizations that want the benefits of incorporating without the expense of creating and maintaining a C-Corporation often consider the S-Corporation business entity. This structure is designed with privately held companies in mind, and it offers reduced personal risk without the steep ongoing expenses associated with C-Corporations. S-Corporations can still have shareholders, but the number is capped at 100. All shareholders must be people, not other businesses. For business owners who have no intention of taking the company public, an S-Corporation provides an excellent balance between risk and reward.

Like C-Corporations, S-Corporations stand alone for legal and tax purposes. Owners are paid a salary, which is taxed as regular income on their personal tax returns. The issue of double taxation that plagues sole proprietors is eliminated. Most important, S-Corporations are fully responsible for debts and legal judgments levied against the business, which protects the owners' personal assets.

Advantages of S-Corporations

- Up to 100 owners and shareholders are permitted
- Full separation between business and personal liability
- Access to some tax deductions and credits reserved for corporations

Disadvantages of S-Corporations

- Significant expense to get started
- Ongoing administrative costs
- Limited number of shareholders
- Inability to access all of the tax deductions and credits available to C-Corporations

Limited Liability Companies (LLC)

When your budget says sole proprietorship, but your legal advisor says corporation, it can be difficult to find balance between keeping expenses low and minimizing risk. Fortunately, there is middle ground. A Limited Liability Company (LLC) could be the right solution for your small business.

This business structure combines the best features of sole proprietorships and partnerships with the most important advantages of corporations. LLCs can operate as independent entities for legal and tax purposes, which may protect your assets against business debts, lawsuits, and the actions of other business owners. It is important to note that this protection is not as comprehensive as that of a C-Corporation.

You can register any size company as an LLC and enjoy significant flexibility as your organization grows and changes. You can file business taxes as you would for an S-Corporation, or you can combine your personal and business taxes the same way sole proprietors or partnerships do. Some LLCs start out with a tax strategy that mirrors sole proprietorship filing methods, and as the business expands and evolves, they transition to a corporate tax strategy. Your Certified Tax Coach is the best resource for designing and executing these strategies.

Advantages of Limited Liability Companies (LLC)

- Businesses of any size can register as an LLC
- Set-up is simple and less costly than other methods of incorporation
- Reduction of personal legal and financial risks
- Ability to adapt tax strategies based on business needs

Disadvantages of Limited Liability Companies (LLC)

- Set-up is more complex and brings higher fees and expenses than sole proprietorships and partnerships
- LLCs are not automatically eligible for the same business deductions and credits that C-Corporations and S-Corporations enjoy
- Personal legal and financial risk is reduced, but it is not completely eliminated

Staying Safe from Excessive Taxes Through Business Entity Selection

There is no perfect solution when it comes to structuring your business. Each of the options for business entities comes with advantages and disadvantages, and your final decision should be based on finding balance. Your business attorney and your Certified Tax Coach are excellent resources as you work through collecting the information relevant to your decision and weighing the possibilities. These professionals can calculate how the potential tax savings associated with each business entity compare to the start-up and administrative expenses.

Finally, as with most financial decisions, doing nothing is rarely the best solution. Failure to take action results in automatic placement in the default business entity: a sole proprietorship or partnership. Be sure to make a decision with your experts and you can avoid needing that life preserver later on.

ABOUT THE AUTHOR

David Auer, CPA, MS, PFS, CGMA, JD, LLM in Taxation, CTC

With over 30 years of experience as a Certified Public Accountant, speaker, best-selling author, business consultant and entrepreneur, David Auer is the Founder and CEO of Provident CPAs.

David is the creator of The Five-S.T.A.R. (Strategic Tax Advice with Results!) Program™, a proactive tax planning strategy for high-income business owners. It allows you to take control of when and how much you pay taxes, creates a strategic roadmap to building tax-free wealth, sets up your business and investments to slash taxes and protect assets, legally lowers your tax in ethical ways so you can sleep at night and not worry about an audit, and finally, gives you peace of mind knowing you have a team of professionals supporting you.

David earned his BSBA and MS in Accounting from Oklahoma State University, his JD from Oklahoma University College of Law, and his LLM in Taxation from New York University School of Law. He has the Personal Financial Specialist (PFS) and Chartered Global Management Accountant (CGMA) designations with the American Institute of CPAs and is a Certified Tax Coach™.

David holds an LLM in Taxation. He is a frequent speaker and is recognized as one of America's Premier Experts®. He is on the adjunct faculty of Asset Protection Corporation, founded by internationally acclaimed asset protection attorney Robert Lambert. David is a member of the National Academy of Best-Selling Authors® and is the author or coauthor of several national best-selling books.

David Auer, CPA, MS, PFS, CGMA, JD, LLM in Taxation, CTC

Provident CPAs

☎ 1-85-LOWER-TAX

📍 9175 S. Yale Avenue, Suite 300 Tulsa, OK 74137

🌐 www.providentcpas.com

✉ info@providentcpas.com

CHAPTER 3

Unsinkable Strategies for Creating Income with Less Tax

JAY MALIK, EA, CTC

O
ne of the most important tax minimization tactics is identifying every possible opportunity to deduct your expenses from your taxable income. However, a truly comprehensive tax minimization strategy approaches the problem from multiple angles. In addition to managing your expenses and applying all appropriate deductions, explore opportunities to generate income that isn't subject to tax in the first place.

Once you have exhausted options for tax-free and tax-deferred revenue, there is still more work to do. Tax rates vary based on how income is produced, and you can realize substantial savings by choosing investments with tax rates in mind. Your Certified Tax Coach is your partner in creating income with lower tax liability.

The Heavy Tax Implications of Common Financial Anchors

Saving and investing in stocks, bonds, and cash equivalents is an important component of your wealth-building strategy. Unfortunately, these products are subject to significant taxation, which lowers your profits dramatically. Understanding how taxes are assessed on your savings and investment accounts is the first step in creating a portfolio the supports your tax minimization goals.

The most popular savings and investment products also tend to be the ones with higher tax rates, and the tax code is written to ensure you pay a percentage of earnings on these products to the IRS. Taxes are assessed whether you choose to withdraw your earnings or you leave them in the account to grow. However, the specific tax rate varies between product types. For example, earnings on some investments are taxed as income, while others are taxed as capital gains. In either case, your ability to minimize your tax bill is limited.

Proceed with caution when investing in the following product types.

Standard Savings Programs

The bank you use for day-to-day expenses wants to expand your relationship beyond a simple checking account. One of the first products your banker will offer is a standard savings account. The interest paid on funds invested in basic savings plans is negligible, but you can withdraw at any time without penalty. Generally, your only restrictions involve the number of withdrawals and electronic transfers you make each month.

Your earnings from a standard savings account are reported on a 1099-INT form, and they are taxed as interest income. When it comes to building your wealth, these savings accounts offer few benefits. However, they are popular because funds are easy to access, and they are FDIC insured up to $250,000.

Money Market Accounts (MMA)

Your financial institution may encourage you to open a Money Market account instead of a standard savings account. This option is a small step up when it comes to earning interest. In exchange for slightly better interest rates, most Money Market products have a higher minimum balance requirement to avoid monthly fees. You are still subject to limits on the number of transactions you make, and your earnings are taxed as interest income. These accounts are also FDIC insured up to $250,000.

Certificates of Deposit (CD)

When you make a commitment to leave funds in your account for a pre-determined period of time, your financial institution is willing to pay a higher rate of interest. The longer you agree to leave your account untouched, the higher the interest rate. Such programs are referred to as Certificates of Deposit or CDs. As with standard savings and Money Market accounts, CD earnings are reported on a 1099-INT and taxed as interest income.

CDs are popular, because they accrue more interest than a standard savings or Money Market account while offering the same level of security. CDs are FDIC insured up to $250,000. The primary risk to investing in a CD is reduced liquidity. If you must withdraw funds before the CD matures, your bank will charge an interest penalty on the withdrawn amount.

Mutual Funds

Inexperienced investors and those with limited funds for their initial deposit often start building wealth through mutual funds. These products offer an opportunity to enjoy the benefits of a diversified investment portfolio without selecting and purchasing individual equities. Investors buy shares of mutual funds, which are directed by a fund manager. The fund manager makes trade decisions, and each share of the mutual fund increases or decreases in value based on the success of these trades.

Although individual investors cannot choose specific stocks when purchasing mutual fund shares, it is possible to choose funds that match investment preferences. Mutual funds are often centered around particular investment strategies or themes. For example, some funds focus on international equities, and others trade exclusively in the area of green energy. Some primarily purchase stock in large companies, while others base trade decisions on maximizing earnings or minimizing risk.

Mutual fund investments are not FDIC insured, so you do face risk in purchasing these shares. However, because your mutual fund shares represent a diverse mix of investments, your risk may be reduced when compared to investing in individual equities.

As the value of underlying investments grows, the value of your mutual fund shares grow, too. Dividends from the underlying investments can increase your total earnings. This makes calculating your tax liability more complicated, because you may be responsible for capital gains taxes, taxes on your dividends, or both. Your Certified Tax Coach has the expertise necessary to steer you safely through this tax storm.

Stock Trading Accounts

Stock trading accounts give you the option of choosing your own investments. You can make trades independently or you can delegate trading to your investment advisor. Stock trading accounts range from basic self-service options, such as those offered by online services like E-Trade, to full-service professionally managed accounts. Fees tend to be lower for self-service accounts, which typically charge a flat rate for each transaction. Full-service accounts often have complex, layered fee structures based on the number of transactions you make and the amount of your investment.

Investments made through stock trading accounts can lose value, whether you choose the self-service or the full-service option. These funds are not FDIC insured. Your tax liability is directly related to the success of your investments. An increase in the value of an individual equity may be subject to capital gains taxes, and you may be responsible for taxes on any dividends you earn.

Lighten the Tax Load with Tax-Advantaged Investment Options

When your goal is to keep your tax bill as low as possible, standard savings and investment products may not be the right choice. None of the accounts listed above offer tax-free or tax-deferred income, unless you pair them with a qualified retirement savings plan. Transitioning a portion of your wealth to tax-advantaged products gives you an opportunity to reduce your taxable income.

The Basics of Tax-Deferred Products

Investing in an asset that offers tax-deferred earnings doesn't absolve you of tax liability forever. At some point, you are expected to pay taxes on the income from these investments. The specific tax rate and timing of your payments depends on the type of investment vehicle you choose. Often, you are required to take distributions after a certain period of time, and taxes are due when you make the withdrawal.

Though taxes must be paid eventually, tax-deferred status gives you more control over when and how much you pay. You have the flexibility of taking distributions and paying taxes in years when your tax rate is lower to reduce the total amount you owe. Two of the most common tax-deferred investments are Traditional IRAs (Individual Retirement Accounts) and annuities.

Traditional IRAs

The government has made a commitment to encouraging individuals to set funds aside for retirement. The Traditional IRA was created to make saving for retirement more appealing. You have the option of contributing your own funds to these IRAs. As long as you don't exceed the annual limit, you can generally deduct your contributions from your taxable income in the year that contributions are made.

Funds held in a Traditional IRA can be invested in a variety of standard products, including certificates of deposit, mutual funds, and stock trading accounts. Taxes on earnings in your IRA enjoy the same deferred status as your principal, so your wealth grows more quickly through the magic of compound interest. When you do take distributions, taxes are assessed on the full amount of your withdrawal. This includes your original contribution as well as your earnings.

Annuities

Certain annuities qualify for tax deferral, so it is worth exploring your options when you design your tax minimization strategy. Unlike other investment options, annuities are insurance products specifically designed to protect against the risk of outliving your retirement savings.

Some investors contribute a lump sum to create their annuity, while others make regular contributions over a predetermined time period. This phase of the annuity can last from a few years to a few decades. Once you reach the total agreed upon investment amount, you don't make any additional deposits. Your money grows until the distribution period begins.

As with the contribution schedule, distribution schedules vary. Depending on the product, you may be able to choose an annuity that pays for a fixed period of time or one that pays regular income until the end of your life, no matter how long you live. If you are willing to accept smaller distributions during your lifetime, you can choose an annuity that provides income for your beneficiaries after your death.

Tax-deferred annuities offer tax advantages that are similar to those of the Traditional IRA. You pay no income tax on the amount you contribute in the year that you make the contribution. Instead, you pay income tax when you take distributions. For many, this means a lower overall tax bill due to a lower tax rate.

Employer Sponsored Retirement Programs

Today's businesses know that retirement planning is a significant concern for most employees, so they offer a retirement savings plan in their compensation and benefits packages. Such programs are not limited to major corporations. Special tax-advantaged retirement savings programs are available for small businesses, and there are options for sole proprietorships as well.

Most employer sponsored retirement programs are designed to defer taxes on contributions. Some permit employers to match employee contributions or to make contributions on behalf of employees using pre-tax income. Taxes are assessed in the year that distributions are taken.

401(k)

The 401(k), named after the section of tax code that created the program, is probably the most well-known employer sponsored retirement account. Many large companies replaced pension programs with 401(k) plans. Instead of contributing to pension accounts, the organizations match employee contributions to their 401(k)s. These plans are complex, and the cost of implementation and administration can be quite high. As a result, they are typically not suitable for small businesses and sole proprietorships.

Contributions are made with pre-tax income, and employees often choose a payroll deduction to automatically transfer funds to their retirement accounts each time they receive a paycheck. This simplifies the process of setting funds aside for retirement and encourages greater participation in the program.

SEP IRA

Small businesses generally find that a 401(k) is not practical. Instead, they take advantage of other tax-advantaged retirement savings plans specifically designed for smaller companies. The Simplified Employee Pension Individual Retirement Account (SEP IRA) offers an opportunity for businesses to make contributions on behalf of their employees without the complexity and expense of a 401(k).

Eligibility for SEP IRA tax advantages depends on a meeting a short list of straightforward criteria. For example, if businesses make contributions to any employee, equivalent contributions must be made for all employees. This includes contributions to the business owner's account, so this option is most popular with sole proprietors.

The SEP IRA offers tax benefits for the company and participating employees. The most popular aspect of a SEP IRA is that employer contributions are not taxed as employee income in the year they are made. As with other tax-deferred retirement savings programs, taxes are assessed when funds are distributed.

SIMPLE IRA

Small businesses with 100 employees or less often find that the Savings Incentive Match Plan for Employees (SIMPLE IRA) is an excellent opportunity to enjoy tax-advantaged retirement savings. Both employers and employees can make tax-deferred contributions.

Employers have a choice between matching a percentage of employees' pay or matching employee contributions. Typically, employers limit contribution matches to a certain percentage of total income. No taxes are due on contributions and earnings until distributions are taken. This reduces tax liability for employers and employees in the year contributions are made.

Solo 401(k)

Individuals who want the benefits of a 401(k) while preserving the freedom of self-employment can choose a special type of 401(k) program. Often referred to as a Solo 401(k), this retirement savings plan is available for self-employed individuals and their spouses, as long as the business has no other employees.

Contribution guidelines are flexible. The business owner can contribute from personal income, the business can contribute from business income, or there can be a combination of both. As with most other retirement savings plans, taxes on contributions are deferred until the account holder takes a withdrawal.

Avoiding the Pitfalls of Early Withdrawal

Tax-deferred retirement savings plans are designed to reward you for setting funds aside until you reach retirement. To ensure that taxpayers don't use these programs inappropriately, there are penalties associated with premature withdrawals.

Funds must remain in the account until you reach the age of 59½, unless you have a financial situation that meets very specific criteria. For example, you may be able to take an early distribution without penalty if you have unexpected medical expenses. If you are not eligible for early withdrawal, you can expect a 10 percent early withdrawal fee in addition to standard income taxes.

If you face unexpected expenses, consult your Certified Tax Coach before tapping into your tax-advantaged retirement savings account. This is particularly important if you have accounts under more than one type of program, as the eligibility criteria for penalty-free early distributions can vary between plans.

Tax-Exempt Investment Options

Tax-deferred programs are quite popular, but they do come with risk. The biggest is the possibility of change in income or tax regulations in the decades between making contributions and taking distributions. Historically, most investors find themselves in lower tax brackets after retirement; however, this is not guaranteed. Fortunately, there are alternative solutions for those unwilling to accept this risk.

Tax-exempt programs eliminate the risk of future tax increases. Contributions are made with after-tax dollars, and funds grow tax-free. When distributions are taken, there is no tax liability. The tax-free status includes both principal and earnings.

Roth IRA

The Roth IRA was created years after the Traditional IRA, and it rapidly caught the attention of investors in search of true tax-free income. It is intended as a retirement savings plan and can cover a wide variety of investment products. After the Roth IRA is established, it serves as an umbrella to protect linked accounts ranging from standard savings plans to full-service trading accounts. Often, participants choose investments that are expected to grow substantially long-term to maximize the tax-free benefits of this program.

There are eligibility criteria you must meet to participate in a Roth IRA. Most notably, there is an income cap for investors. If you make more than a certain amount each year, you are not eligible for this type of tax-free income. The income threshold is reviewed regularly, and it changes with the economy as appropriate.

Contributions for those who qualify are made with after-tax dollars up to a pre-determined threshold. The cap is reviewed annually and rises to keep pace with the economic landscape. You cannot exceed the yearly Roth IRA maximum contribution. Interest and earnings compound and the total balance grows, but no tax is assessed when withdrawals are taken according to the program guidelines.

Because the tax advantages are intended to encourage retirement savings, you cannot take distributions before the age of 59½ unless you face a specific type of financial hardship. If you choose to withdraw funds outside of program guidelines, you will be taxed on the earnings. However, taxes on your contributions are already paid, and you will never be taxed a second time on that portion of your distribution.

Life Insurance

Many employees are covered by employer-sponsored life insurance, and some purchase additional coverage in the form of short-term life policies. Typically, these are intended to cover final expenses and funeral costs. However, with careful planning, it is possible to leverage the power of life insurance to boost your tax-free income.

Term life insurance works like other standard policies, including homeowner's insurance and auto insurance. You pay a pre-determined amount based on the value of your property and the level of risk you present to the insurer, and you receive reimbursement in case of a covered loss. Once the policy's term expires, coverage ends. There is no lasting value.

Whole life insurance, also known as universal life insurance, is a true investment. By purchasing this type of policy, you have an opportunity to gain tax-free income. Like term life insurance, your beneficiaries receive the proceeds of your policy in case of your death, so they can cover final expenses and supplement household income. Unlike term life insurance, the policy builds value over time.

Each time you make a payment for your whole or universal policy, a portion of the premium is invested. This translates into cash that you can access when financial need arises. While these policies are considerably more expensive than term insurance, they offer lasting value that is not matched by term policies.

In most cases, you continue to make payments on whole policies for as long as you own them; however, there are products that set a limit on how many payments you can make. After you have completed the full payment schedule, which may range from 10–25 years, your protection and the policy's cash value remain in force for the remainder of your lifetime.

Life insurance does not have the same income limits that impact the Roth IRA program. You can choose this option in addition to your Roth IRA or instead of a Roth IRA if you do not fit Roth IRA eligibility criteria.

Annuities

When it comes to tax minimization, annuities play an important role. As mentioned previously, some types offer the opportunity to defer taxes until payments begin. Certain annuities are designed to take tax reduction a step further by creating true tax-free income.

As with other types of tax-free income programs, contributions to annuities are made with after-tax dollars. When the payment phase begins, no income tax is assessed on the portion of the distributions that has already been taxed. This translates into significant tax savings during a period when you might also be taking distributions from tax-deferred accounts.

Annuity programs can often be customized to meet your individual needs, so discuss the best way to optimize contributions with your Certified Tax Coach. You can pay into an annuity over time or with a lump sum, and you can choose when and how to receive payments. For example, some programs guarantee income for the remainder of your life, ensuring you do not outlive your savings. There are also options that make payments to your surviving spouse or other beneficiaries, assuring them of tax-free income after you are gone.

If your goal is to increase your tax-free income, an annuity can play an important role in your success. Unlike Roth IRAs, there is no income limit for participating in annuity programs, and there is no cap on the amounts of your contributions. You can pass funds on to your beneficiaries directly, saving the time and expense of probate. Finally, if you choose an annuity that offers you a guaranteed death benefit, you are assured that your beneficiaries will receive a pre-determined amount, regardless of how well your investments perform.

Transitioning to Tax-Free Income

Tax-deferred accounts such as employer-sponsored 401(k)s are widely available. Many new investors choose these over the less understood tax-free options. Later, they realize they would be better served by a tax-free product, such as a Roth IRA. Fortunately, you can transition your savings from tax-deferred to tax-free accounts with the help of a Conversion Roth IRA.

It is worth noting that as of 2010, there are no income limits for the Conversion Roth IRA. As a result, you might hear it referred to as a "backdoor" Roth IRA. Some investors who exceed the income limits for creating a standard Roth IRA make contributions to a tax-deferred account and transition to a tax-free account using the Conversion Roth IRA.

If you have determined that your tax minimization strategy requires more tax-free income, the Conversion Roth IRA might be right for you. Work with your Certified Tax Coach to complete the process as quickly as possible, so that your earnings can begin to grow tax-free.

Integrating Social Security Benefits with Your Tax-Free Income Strategy

Because your Social Security benefits add to your income during the same period that you are likely to take distributions from tax-deferred and tax-free investments, it is important to understand how they impact your tax liability. Social Security is partially tax-free, but the additional income can affect the rate at which other income is taxed.

The most effective tactic for keeping your taxes low is to wait as long as possible before you begin taking Social Security payments. The monthly amount you receive is calculated using a formula that compares when you start taking payments with your life expectancy. The earlier you start taking payments, the lower each payment will be.

You can keep your taxes low by taking distributions from tax-deferred accounts first. Once those funds are exhausted, you can combine your Social Security benefits with distributions from Roth IRAs and other tax-free accounts. The effect is a reduction in your taxable income, so your tax liability is as low as possible long-term.

If you are serious about minimizing your taxes long-term, a single tactic simply won't do the job. True tax minimization requires a comprehensive strategy that combines the tax-saving possibilities of multiple investment options.

Tax-deferred accounts are important for saving on taxes today. They may also offer income with minimal tax liability in the future, when your total taxable income is lower. Tax-free programs are critical to the overall success of your strategy, as they give your investments an opportunity to grow without incurring any tax liability.

Your Certified Tax Coach and the other members of your financial advisory team are your lifeguards when it comes to avoiding high tax bills. These professionals have a variety of tools and techniques to guide you safely through dangerous, tax-infested financial waters.

ABOUT THE AUTHOR

Jay Malik, EA, CTC

Jay Malik is an author and speaker specializing in money matters for dentists. He is the inventor of The R.I.C.H. Dentist System℠, an integrated set of protocols to help dentists achieve a fulfilled life without anxiety about money. His practice as a Money Coach, Accountant, Tax Strategist, and Wealth Advisor serves dentists throughout the US and has helped them implement The R.I.C.H. Dentist System℠ to achieve a stress-free life, one that is prosperity driven and ultimately leads to financial freedom.

Jay teaches The R.I.C.H. Dentist System℠ at conferences and seminars organized by different associations, societies, and study groups of dentists all over the US. He has successfully coached hundreds of dentists out of difficult financial situations including high debt, consequences of bad investments, divorces, and dissolution of partnerships. Specializing in working with health professionals, Jay understands the unique perspective of doctors, their working conditions, and the restrictions they face in managing their money. Jay has developed systems and protocols to deal with such challenges in effective ways.

Jay's system is focused on helping dentists keep more of the money they make by reducing their tax burden through employing an advanced tax planning process and implementing creative techniques that take advantage of the latest court decisions and IRS rulings. He develops and implements proactive individualized tax and financial plans to increase the net wealth of his clients in a holistic manner without compromising quality of life. Jay's clients have saved up to 67% in tax in the first year of working with him by introducing such plans.

Jay Malik, EA, CTC

Less Tax for Dentists

📞 305-563-6000

📍 218 Commercial Blvd, Suite 208, Lauderdale By The Sea, FL 33308

🌐 www.LessTaxForDentists.com

✉ info@lesstaxfordentists.com

CHAPTER 4

Sheltering Your Home-Based Business from the Tax Deluge

ALEXIS E. GALLATI, EA, MBA, MS TAX, CTC

Whether you ease into entrepreneurship by adding a side gig or you plunge all the way into small business ownership, working for yourself is both thrilling and terrifying. You enjoy the benefits of being your own boss, and you can pursue your passion from the comfort of your own home. Of course, there are disadvantages to small business ownership, too. You must take on a long list of new responsibilities like marketing, customer service, and paying bills. One of your most critical tasks is creating a plan to minimize your taxes. If you skip this step, you may face a downpour of unexpected expenses when you file your returns.

Your Certified Tax Coach offers protection against the tax storm. These are some of the lifesaving techniques you can leverage to improve your profits while keeping your tax bill low.

Testing the Entrepreneurial Waters

Home-based businesses are popular with those testing the waters of the entrepreneurial world, because some of the risks of launching a start-up are eliminated. Your overhead expenses are lower when you don't have to lease office space and/or a storefront, so you can still meet your financial obligations while sales are ramping up.

The primary drawback to home-based businesses is that they tend to require longer ramp up periods before generating a profit. This may not be a problem if you are balancing a regular job with your new company, because your transition from the traditional world of work to being your own boss can take place gradually.

You will maximize your chances of success by choosing the right type of business for your temperament and your personal circumstances. These are a few of the questions to consider before committing.

- What personality traits are needed for running a home-based business? Are you confident that you are a good match?
- What type of business makes the most sense based on your current situation and your interests?
- Are there tax regulations and other laws that impact your potential company?

Going through the exercise of answering these questions gives you a starting point for the planning phase of your business. You can narrow down your options to a few that are most likely to be successful, and you have an opportunity to identify and mitigate potential risks early in the process.

Introvert vs. Extrovert: What Characteristics Are Required for Success?

It seems that anyone who has dipped a toe in the waters of a home-based business venture has an opinion about the characteristics and traits required for success. Some insist that you must be an introvert to thrive on the isolation of a non-traditional work environment. Others maintain that only extroverts have the right personality to develop relationships with their customers. There is even a vocal group that asserts it is simply not possible to be productive from a home office, regardless of the characteristics of your personality.

In truth, all of these views are inaccurate. Both introverts and extroverts have founded extremely successful home-based businesses. Introverts often discover they have more energy to manage important business relationships because they don't expend their limited resources on the constant interactions of an office environment. Extroverts leverage their outgoing personalities to make strong connections. They can build relationships from anywhere, whether in an office, through video conferencing, or over the phone.

Studies have demonstrated that many people are more productive from home, particularly when they are highly engaged in their work. Home-based distractions aren't necessarily more disruptive than the distractions that regularly occur in an office setting, and it is common for home-based entrepreneurs to offset interruptions by putting in extra time during evenings and weekends. In fact, the additional flexibility generally reduces stress and anxiety related to being away from family for long hours, which leads to better work/life balance and greater productivity.

If success doesn't depend on being an introvert or an extrovert, what are the necessary characteristics? First and most important, you must be able to adapt quickly as circumstances change. Even the most carefully planned strategies are sure to hit a few bumps along the way, and you must be able to adjust and respond effectively.

Enthusiasm for continuous learning is a plus for entrepreneurs. Every week there are developments in technology, and there is a constant supply of new ideas for managing your business more efficiently, more profitably, and more resourcefully. If you are open to developing new skills and applying new strategies, you will have a significant edge over the competition.

Finally, it's important that you love what you do. Your business may be a passion project based on a long-held dream, or you might be inspired by the very act of owning and managing your own company, regardless of the industry. Either way, you have to be motivated to achieve long-term success, because you will put in long hours and hard work before you see results.

Building a Home-Based Business That Inspires

The digital transformation has completely changed how owners and their businesses form relationships with consumers, and e-commerce is growing at a dizzying pace. At one time, opportunities for home-based businesses were limited to direct sales companies like Avon and Tupperware. In today's digital marketplace, there are few limits on the goods and services you can offer from your home. If you don't already have a product or service in mind, you may be overwhelmed by your options.

If you are in this category, there are plenty of resources to help you through the planning process, but you need to do some work on your own first. Start by listing your passions, then add your areas of experience. Your list should also include the skills and abilities you already have. Brainstorm to create a collection of business ideas that match one or more of the passions, experience, skills, and abilities on your list.

Next, do some research to determine whether any of your business ideas are viable. A wide variety of magazines, books, and websites are dedicated to choosing a small business and launching a startup. Are other entrepreneurs succeeding in this area?

Spend some time networking online and in person. Join groups associated with your potential industry and connect with local small business and entrepreneurship associations. There is no need to rush the process of selecting the type of company you want to run. Wait until you identify an opportunity that blends well with your lifestyle, your interests, and your current skills.

Keep in mind that plenty of home-based businesses are based on goods and services that people use every day. You don't have to come up with a brand new product or a one-of-a-kind idea to be successful. If your passion is being your own boss, perhaps you can create a business from the skills developed in your current career. For example, after years of working as a staff therapist, you may decide to open your own practice.

Finally, as you research opportunities, you might discover that owning your own business is not your true goal. Your actual objective is to achieve a better work/life balance through home-based employment. In this situation, there is no need to take on the stressors of entrepreneurship. Instead, you may wish to explore opportunities with companies that are open to virtual employees and remote independent contractors. While these positions are available in nearly every area of specialization, some types of remote jobs are harder to find than others. You will have the most luck if you are available for customer service, technical support, and sales.

Tips for Avoiding Sharks, Con Artists, and Frauds

As you are researching home-based business opportunities, you are sure to come across listings that sound too good to be true. Unfortunately, forums for home-based business networking are popular with sharks, con artists, and frauds. Too-good-to-be-true offers are often the first sign of a swindle. These scams promise to provide you everything you need to launch a profitable business, but there is a catch. You must pay an up-front fee to access business materials. Sometimes, you pay the fee and receive nothing in return. Other times, the package you receive isn't at all what was promised. In either case, there is no recourse, and you are unlikely to get a refund.

Direct sales companies aren't necessarily a scam. A number of legitimate organizations offer these sorts of opportunities, but you must proceed with caution. Even when the company is reputable and you receive the materials as promised, making a profit is less common than marketing would have you believe. Profitability depends on convincing friends and family members to buy product from you and to open businesses of their own. If you aren't comfortable with these sales methods or the market is already saturated with the product, you could find yourself stuck with lots of merchandise and no money.

The bottom line is that investing in any business opportunity that offers massive profits with minimal effort is not wise. If it sounds like a get rich quick scheme, it probably is. Don't send a dime until you have thoroughly researched the organization through consumer watchdog groups like the Better Business Bureau and the Federal Trade Commission's online consumer site. Social media can be a valuable source of information on these companies as well. Join groups devoted to the topic or look through ratings and feedback to better understand the pros and cons of any business you are considering.

Finally, under no circumstances should you release any sensitive personal information until you have completed your research and you are convinced that the company is legitimate. Fraudulent business opportunities aren't always designed to collect sign-up fees. Some are built to accumulate personal data for identity theft and other illegal schemes.

Buying an Established Home-Based Business or Franchise

When your primary goal is to work for yourself, but you don't want the stress of building from the ground up, there are options that offer the best of both worlds. If you like the idea of leveraging the marketing resources of a larger organization, purchasing a franchise might be right for you. If you prefer an independent company that comes complete with an established consumer base, you can buy an existing home-based business. Instead of starting from nothing, you simply transition existing infrastructure and clients from the current owner to yourself.

Before you commit to buying an existing home-based business, complete the same detailed research required for purchasing a traditional business. Review financial records and examine the company's competitors, reputation, and client list. Make sure you understand why the current owner wants to sell. If the current owner is unable to generate profits, consider how you would do things differently and whether you could turn the business around before signing a purchase agreement.

A franchise offers many of the benefits of purchasing an existing home-based business without the related baggage. You pay a franchise fee, which gives you access to a trusted business name, an established reputation, and a variety of tools, training, and support to ensure your launch is successful.

You are the owner of a franchise business, but in exchange for the established reputation and corporate support, you are required to observe franchise rules. Before committing, examine the fine print with your attorney and your Certified Tax Coach. This step ensures you understand your obligations to the parent company, as well as the tax ramifications of buying into the business.

Structuring Your Business to Keep Taxes Low

Unless you take specific action, your home-based business will default to a sole proprietorship structure. However, from a long-term perspective, this may not be the best business entity for legal and tax purposes. The disadvantages of sole proprietorships should be carefully considered before you move forward.

Sole proprietorships put you in a situation where there is minimal separation between personal and business income. When the business operates from your home, the line between personal and business affairs gets even fuzzier. Under this structure, you can be held personally responsible if your business gets into legal or financial trouble and vice versa.

The tax implications of a sole proprietorship should not be ignored. When your personal and business finances are intertwined, you often pay more in taxes than you would under other business structures. Sole proprietors pay both self-employment taxes and income taxes on business profits, which can add up to a large quarterly bill. Your Certified Tax Coach will assist with reviewing all of your options so you can choose the business entity that keeps tax expense as low as possible.

Alternative business entities such as a Limited Liability Companies (LLC) and S-Corporations offer greater protection from legal and financial risk. Through these structures, you may avoid situations in which your business liabilities carry over to your personal finances. These alternative business entities are completely separate from your personal identity for tax purposes. They have unique tax identification numbers, and they are responsible for the taxes associated with business profits. The key is maintaining a clear separation between personal and professional finances. However, this can be tricky when you operate the business from your home. If intermingling starts to occur, you could lose the legal and financial protections of owning an LLC or corporation.

Regulatory Issues for Home-Based Businesses

Selecting the type of business you wish to own and the most appropriate business entity are major steps forward, but there is still work to be done before you make your first sale. The next step is to become familiar with local, state, and federal business regulations that could impact your company. Even though your business is based out of your home, you are subject to standard employment and tax laws. In addition, there may be legal requirements specific to your industry or to home-based businesses in your area.

Learn about the following regulations that are most likely to affect your company.

Zoning and Permitting

Real estate is divided into zones that indicate what sort of activities can take place in a given area. Examples include commercial, residential, and industrial zones. Though some zones permit residential, commercial, and/or industrial real estate in close proximity, combining these activities in the same building isn't always allowed. For example, people generally cannot reside in buildings zoned for industrial use.

Even if it seems that your business is subject to zoning regulations that prevent you from opening your theoretical doors, there may be exceptions to the regulations for operating small professional practices or other types of home-based businesses from a single family property. In some cases, the specifics of these exceptions are spelled out in the zoning ordinances. However, it is more common for each exception to go through an approval process. In most cities and towns, you must participate in a hearing before your request is granted. Either way, it is important to have appropriate permits on hand before you begin operations.

Licensing

If your profession requires a license to practice outside of the home, you are required to hold that license for a home-based business as well. For example, massage therapists, daycare providers, and accountants must be licensed, regardless of when and how they provide services. Unfortunately, many entrepreneurs launching home-based practices neglect this critical step. This omission can lead to serious legal, financial, and professional consequences.

Employment Laws

Under federal, state, and local employment laws, employees are afforded certain rights and protections. For example, some cities and states have initiated paid sick leave requirements, and there are national regulations around minimum wage and child labor. Many employment laws exclude small businesses, so you may be exempt from certain responsibilities. However, if you have any employees, it is best to review all major employment regulations to be sure you are in compliance.

Copyright Regulations

Company names, symbols, and other branding elements are crucial to marketing efforts, and organizations of every size guard this type of intellectual property carefully. No matter how small your home-based business is, you can be sure that you will hear from your competitors if you infringe on their brand. Do some research before you settle on a specific name, logo, and tagline for your business. This gives you an opportunity to validate that your selections are completely original and that you have established a legal right to use them.

Business Insurance: Your Financial Life Vest

You already know how important it is to maintain homeowner's insurance, vehicle insurance, and life insurance. These policies protect you and your loved ones from a catastrophic loss. When you launch a home-based business, you may need additional insurance protection. Your personal policies don't necessarily cover business losses. Your financial advisor can give you details on the most appropriate insurance for your particular situation. There are several types of insurance to consider.

Medical Insurance

If you decided to go all in with your new venture and you have left your day job, you may find yourself without medical insurance. Some entrepreneurs can be added to their spouse's policy, and others rely on COBRA while they get their company off the ground. You also have the option of purchasing an individual policy from health insurance providers operating in your state. In many cases, you can shop for these policies through an online database.

Because COBRA and individual policies are not subsidized by your employer, they represent a significant expense. You may be tempted to forgo health insurance and hope for the best, but this is a risky decision. Unpaid medical bills are a leading cause of bankruptcy, and the costs associated with even minor illnesses and accidents can be thousands of dollars. Without insurance, this sort of setback can disrupt your budget for months.

Property Insurance

When you own a home-based business, it is common to assume that your standard homeowner's insurance policy will cover business losses if you have damage due to fire, flood, theft, or another emergency. Unfortunately, that is often not the case. Many policies specifically exclude business assets, even if they are located in your home when the loss occurs.

Speak with your agent to better understand what your current homeowner's policy covers, then consider separate property insurance to cover losses related to your home-based business. You may also benefit from liability insurance to protect your customers, suppliers, and employees.

The same principles apply to the insurance you carry on your personal vehicles. These policies may also exclude losses incurred during business-related activities.

Business Interruption and Disability Insurance

It's exciting when your business is successful and you see your profits rising. However, the more you rely on the income from your home-based business, the more vulnerable you are to any issues that interfere with operations and affect income. If you fall ill or a natural disaster interrupts your work, you could find yourself in a financial bind.

Business interruption insurance and disability insurance are designed to protect against these sorts of disruptions, so that you have income continuity if issues outside of your control prevent you from working. Although business interruption insurance and disability insurance might not be necessary when you are just starting out, they are important items to include when you conduct periodic financial reviews.

These three types of insurance are often a priority for home-based business owners, but there are a variety of other protections that may be necessary depending on your industry and the specific work you do. For example, professional service providers such as attorneys and healthcare practitioners typically need malpractice insurance. Companies that perform services inside clients' homes may need to be bonded against theft. Your financial advisor, insurance agent, business attorney, and relevant professional organizations are helpful resources for determining the best policies for your situation.

Keeping the Business Tax Deluge in Check

One of the primary reasons many entrepreneurs choose a home-based business model is to reduce overhead expenses. However, there are other ways your home-based business can save you money. For example, operating your company from your residence may qualify you for exclusive tax deductions and credits on your personal returns. The home office tax deduction is particularly valuable, because it offsets some of the costs associated with owning and maintaining your home.

The home office tax deduction has become even more important under the new tax reform laws because there are now fewer deductions available for individuals who itemize. Through this option, you have an opportunity to deduct a portion of your utility bills, home depreciation, mortgage interest, and repair and maintenance expenses. The impact to your final tax bill may be significant, so it is worth examining your eligibility.

The IRS requires that you meet the following criteria to qualify for a home office tax deduction:

- The home office is used for business purposes only.
- It is used on a regular basis.
- The home office is either your principle place of business, or it regularly functions as a meeting place for you and your clients.

Many people believe they are not eligible for this deduction because of the requirement that home offices are used exclusively for business. Unfortunately, there are few exceptions to this rule. In rare circumstances, such as with a home daycare, you may qualify for the home office deduction despite the fact that the children in your care spend time throughout the house.

The substantial savings available through the home office deduction usually make the loss of leisure space worthwhile. This life preserver has the potential to rescue you from steep tax bills, so be sure to discuss the pros and cons with your Certified Tax Coach.

A home-based business offers the best of both worlds. You can enjoy the excitement and independence of launching your own company, while still maintaining a regular job to keep your finances stable if necessary. Because you don't have to leave the house to operate your new business, you can minimize disruption to your work/life balance. Best of all, a home-based business gives you access to lifesaving tax reduction techniques that will help you improve your profits while keeping your tax bill low.

ABOUT THE AUTHOR

Alexis E. Gallati, EA, MBA, MS Tax, CTC

After over 12 successful years working for certified public accounting firms, Alexis Gallati founded Gallati Professional Services in 2014, specializing in comprehensive tax planning and compliance for accomplished medical, dental, and veterinary professionals and their businesses. Not only does she have extensive experience in over 400 tax planning strategies and multistate tax preparation, but she has trained at the highest level, holding two master's degrees (Master of Business Administration and Master of Science in Taxation), and serves as an Enrolled Agent, NTPI Fellow, and Certified Tax Coach.

Growing up in a family of physicians, and later marrying a physician, Alexis understands how much hard work healthcare professionals put in to operating a successful practice. She also sees how often other advisors try to take advantage of their successes, siphoning away their money and not creating wealth. That's why she's here to be a confidant, someone her clients can trust to give them sound tax advice.

With the guidance of Alexis, her clients save on average 47% annually in tax and use that money toward their financial and personal goals such as investing back into their business, saving for retirement, or taking that much needed vacation. Her clients also enjoy consistent and proactive communication throughout the year and the use of top technology to make working with Alexis as easy as possible.

When she's not busy helping her clients succeed, she spends her time with her wonderful husband and their four children. She is also an avid equestrian and enjoys learning new technologies.

Alexis E. Gallati, EA, MBA, MS Tax, CTC

Gallati Professional Services

📞 865-281-1461

📍 9111 Cross Park Drive Ste D200 Knoxville, TN 37923

🌐 www.GallatiTax.com

✉️ agallati@gallatitax.com

CHAPTER 5

Sunken Treasure: The Business Deductions You Are Probably Missing

LUKE GHEEN, MBA, CPA, CTC

The tax code is extraordinarily complex, and new case law develops every year. Keeping up with all of the deductions available to business owners is a full-time job. Unfortunately, even the best accountants struggle to stay current, as they are primarily focused on routine tax matters. Their priority is ensuring complete, accurate returns for a large volume of clients.

No matter how diligent you are about tracking expenses and saving receipts, you probably aren't getting all of the tax savings you could. Your Certified Tax Coach is dedicated to ensuring you claim every deduction you are entitled to. With the help of a professional, you can identify hidden treasure and lower your tax bill, so more of your wealth stays in your pocket. Some of the tax deductions you may be missing are uncovered here.

Avoid the Danger Zone

Before discussing more sophisticated tax minimization strategies, a word of caution: stay inside the boundaries of the law. The consequences of swimming beyond the IRS safety rope could be catastrophic. You can get caught up in a tangle of legal and financial consequences, including fines, penalties, interest, even jail time.

Keep in mind that loopholes are written into the tax code to encourage specific behaviors. For example, there are a variety of deductions available to nurture small business growth. Application of these techniques is carefully monitored to prevent improper use. Your Certified Tax Coach will help you differentiate between making the most of legal loopholes that allow you to save on taxes and exploiting the system with illegal tax maneuvers that will draw unwanted attention.

Little-Known Expense Deductions

If your business is like most, standard deductions like utilities and rent are already on your tax return. However, these basic costs are just the tip of the iceberg when it comes to business expenses. You are spending far more to keep operations running smoothly, and there is a strong possibility that other business-related activities will qualify for additional tax savings.

Before you spend another dime, create a process for recording each and every expense. Once you see where your money is going, you can work with your Certified Tax Coach to maximize your deductions. Business owners often overlook many opportunities; review the following categories to see what might apply to you.

Costs of Maintaining a Home Office

Running a company requires round-the-clock availability, and you are probably called upon at all hours to resolve employee and customer concerns. Chances are, there is an area in your home specifically dedicated to business activities. If not, it is worthwhile to establish one. Even if you already have space set aside on the premises of your business, you can deduct expenses associated with a home office on your personal tax returns.

When you have a home office, you can deduct a percentage of the costs associated with owning or renting your dwelling. For example, a portion of your utilities and mortgage or rent are likely to qualify. This reduces your personal tax liability, saving you money that would otherwise go to the IRS.

Special Savings for Startups

Building a business takes a lot of money up-front. There is equipment and inventory to buy, and you must invest in marketing to attract the first wave of clients. As a result, many entrepreneurs never get beyond developing a business plan. They realize they simply can't afford to launch a company once they complete their initial financial assessment.

The government takes a particular interest in promoting the growth of new businesses because these companies create jobs and strengthen the economy. In an effort to offset some of the financial burden associated with launching a startup, a special tax savings opportunity was created. In your first year of operation, you can deduct up to $10,000 of your startup and organizational costs.

Eligible expenses include basics like equipment and inventory, as well as any fees paid to establish your business structure. This is particularly helpful for S-Corporations and Limited Liability Companies (LLCs) that face higher fees than similarly sized sole proprietorships and partnerships. If you incur expenses during the initial research and planning phase of your startup, you may be able to deduct those as well. For example, costs associated with developing a more effective product to compete with items already on the market may qualify under this regulation.

More Support for Startups

The $10,000 deduction for startup expenses isn't the only opportunity available to new business owners. You also have the option of accelerating depreciation on some of your equipment. As you probably know, most of the assets that you purchase to support income generation are depreciated over several years. For example, manufacturing tools are depreciated over three years, computers over five years, and furniture over seven years.

Under this special exception, you can depreciate the entire cost of certain equipment in the first year. Note that this option is only available for assets that were new when you bought them, and there is a limit to the amount that you can deduct in a single year. If you exceed the cap, you can deduct remaining depreciation over time, just as you will for future purchases.

As you consider whether these deductions make sense for your business, consult your Certified Tax Coach to ensure you are using the appropriate start date under IRS regulations. Tax code defines your company's official start date as the date you have everything needed to create the product or perform the service you are selling, and you are available to create the products and perform the services if called upon to do so. This start date applies whether you have customers or not.

For example, if you open a car wash but no one comes in until the third day, your business start date is still the first day you were open for business. If you are a graphic designer and you are available for work, but it takes weeks to engage a client, your start date is still the first day you were ready to take assignments.

Tax Deductions for Business Vehicles

As with any major equipment purchase, the best time to consult with your Certified Tax Coach is before you buy a vehicle. The decision to buy versus lease can impact your tax liability, and cars and light trucks offer smaller tax benefits than their larger counterparts. Bigger tax deductions are typically available for vehicles over 6,000 pounds, so you may discover that the extra cost of a full-size pickup or van is worthwhile once you calculate tax savings. For context, the curb weight of an average midsize car is approximately 3,500 pounds, while a full-size truck or SUV weighs 5,500 pounds or more.

Expenses Related to Branding and Marketing

Getting the word out about your new business is a big focus in your first year. After all, it doesn't matter how good your products and services are if nobody knows about them. In addition to traditional advertising methods such as billboards, radio, and print, digital marketing offers extensive opportunities to make connections with your target demographic.

Creating digital content like articles, images, and videos is critical for attracting clientele. When added to must-haves like business cards and brochures, marketing quickly gets expensive. Fortunately, many of these expenses are tax-deductible. The basic costs of marketing materials aren't your only opportunity for tax savings. You may also be able to include expenses associated with hiring professional graphic designers, content creators, videographers, and similar. Your Certified Tax Coach can tell you more about which expenses are—and are not—deductible.

Lowering Taxes with Training and Development

Building a business from the ground up requires a specialized skill set, but you need an entirely separate set of skills to manage the organization for long-term success. Though you probably already have a solid base of knowledge, continuous learning can ensure you overcome unexpected obstacles.

Some entrepreneurs pass up training and development opportunities such as classes, workshops, and seminars because the associated expense just doesn't fit their budget. Fortunately, tax regulations are designed to make learning affordable. The costs of training and development are often tax deductible, and that's not all. You may be able to write off your investment in books, trade magazine subscriptions, and dues paid to professional organizations as well, if you can show they are relevant to your work.

Investments in Health and Wellness

It goes without saying that the healthier you are, the easier it is to keep up with the demands of a growing business. This principle also applies to your employees. If your company is set up as a corporation, your investment in wellness equipment and programming can pay off in more ways than one. In addition to improving your own health and that of your staff, maintenance costs associated with wellness equipment may be tax deductible. This applies to equipment that is available for all employees to use.

This area of tax law changes frequently, so your Certified Tax Coach is an important resource. Check in to be sure that you are still eligible for deductions you used in previous years and explore new benefits that can be applied to your business returns.

Bringing Family on Board

One of the greatest joys of owning your own company is the opportunity to work side-by-side with your loved ones. Many small business owners rely on their spouse and children to manage day-to-day operations. Parents enjoy extra time with their kids, and they have a chance to pass along critical life skills. Children get a chance to earn their own money while learning the inner workings of the business world.

And when you hire family members to work for your company, you get more than quality time together. If your employees are also dependents, you may qualify for significant tax savings. There are some nuances to claiming these types of tax benefits, so be sure to connect with your Certified Tax Coach before hiring family members.

Retirement Accounts

Setting funds aside for retirement is a financial priority, and business owners have a variety of options for tax-advantaged accounts. When your spouse is also your employee, you have even more opportunities to save. Both you and your spouse can continue to contribute to traditional IRAs, Roth IRAs, or plans sponsored through your company. You will enjoy the standard tax savings that come with these plans, and your business can take deductions for contributions made on behalf of both you and your spouse.

Medicare and Social Security Taxes

Sole proprietorships and small businesses in which you and your spouse are the only partners have a special opportunity to save on Medicare and Social Security taxes by hiring your minor children to perform age-appropriate tasks. Because they are under the age of 18, the business may realize substantial tax savings.

Unemployment Taxes

There is a long list of taxes businesses must pay to protect their employees, and unemployment taxes can be among the most costly. If you have children under the age of 21, you can hire them to work for your company, and you may be able to avoid the taxes you would otherwise pay for non-family employees. You can also avoid unemployment taxes if your spouse is an employee of the business. This benefit is only applicable to organizations that have no non-family owners, so it is most commonly used by sole proprietors.

Bringing family on board may be an opportunity to save on taxes, but you will only benefit if they are performing legitimate tasks that are necessary for business operations. The IRS carefully examines job titles and responsibilities when business owners hire their children, and you can expect hefty penalties if you try to slide under the radar.

Make sure that job titles and related activities match your family members' education and experience. For example, your 17-year-old is probably not qualified for an engineering role, but he can be employed as an engineering assistant. The rate of pay you offer your family members must be appropriate for the job title. As a clerk, your 18-year-old daughter shouldn't receive a salary that is greater than your Marketing Director's.

Auditors tend to look very carefully at family members' job titles, responsibilities, and pay, so be sure you stay well within the safety zone when hiring your children. Protect yourself and your family members by keeping detailed records of the work they do. If there is any question about the legitimacy of their positions, you will have the documentation necessary to back up your deductions.

Reducing Taxes Through Reward and Recognition

When your employees are engaged in their work, turnover goes down and productivity goes up. One of the most important methods of creating a positive, engaging culture is recognizing a job well done. Your staff also appreciates when you remember important milestones such as birthdays and anniversaries. A small token of gratitude goes a long way toward building loyalty.

Most business owners cover reward and recognition expenses from their own pockets, but that's not necessary. From a tax perspective, your company may benefit from deducting these types of costs. Small business owners often miss opportunities to save on reward and recognition; consider the examples below.

Showing Appreciation on Service Anniversaries

Employees take note of their years of service, and it gives them a boost when you notice their commitment to the organization. You may be able to deduct the cost of length of service awards if you give a gift instead of cash. The item must be valued at $400 or less, and you are limited to one gift per employee every five years. This offers plenty of room for creativity, as you can send flowers, present a piece of jewelry or a watch, or give staff members a selection of items from which to choose.

Making an Impression with Meals and Snacks

Though your employees will certainly welcome gifts, the best way to their hearts is through food. A congratulatory lunch or surprise morning pastries make a lasting impression on your staff. While you won't be able to deduct these expenses if you go overboard with quantity and cost, you may be able to save on taxes when you supply your staff with reasonable meals and snacks.

Celebrating Special Occasions

Every company has its own birthday traditions, and some are more elaborate than others. Some business owners buy employees lunch to celebrate their day, while others recognize the occasion with cake and ice cream for everyone. Though it is common for business leaders to cover these costs out-of-pocket, they may be deductible business expenses. In general, non-cash gifts valued at less than $25 will qualify.

Birthdays aren't the only opportunity to celebrate. You can also apply this deduction when you recognize other important life events. For example, employees appreciate your thoughtfulness when you give small gifts to celebrate a wedding or the birth of a child.

Attracting and retaining top talent is a challenge in today's bustling labor market and focusing on employee engagement is no longer optional. Reward and recognition are an important part of any comprehensive engagement strategy, and they bring the extra benefit of saving you money on taxes.

Day-to-Day Activities that May Be Deductible

There are costs associated with nearly everything you do for your company, from connecting with current and prospective clients to overseeing remote business operations. The small outlays you make on a daily basis quickly add up to significant expense. Unfortunately, most business owners fail to strategize when it comes to these minor transactions, so they miss out on opportunities to reduce their tax liability. With a few tweaks, you can increase your deductible expenses substantially, resulting in long-term savings on taxes. Check out the opportunities that follow.

Business-Related Meals and Entertainment

Think through your daily routine and consider how often you stop for a cup of coffee or buy lunch from the corner sandwich shop. When you go alone, these expenses are entirely personal. However, if you invite a current or potential client along, the situation changes. As long as business is a topic of conversation at some point before, during, or after the meal, 50 percent of this expense is usually tax deductible.

The same principle applies to inviting an employee to join you for coffee or dinner. If you spend some of your time talking shop, you can save on your tax bill. Though each outing represents a small expense, the total adds up over time. By the end of the year, your total tax liability may decrease substantially.

Making Leisure Time Profitable

Launching a business is often the result of turning your passion into profit, and there are many entrepreneurs operating companies centered around their hobbies. Your leisure activities may lend themselves to some sort of business arrangement. If you can find the right combination of passion and profit, expenses related to your hobby may be tax deductible.

For example, crafting is a popular pastime, and there is a market for all sorts of handmade items. Even if you primarily knit for fun, consider occasionally selling your handiwork through handmade shopping sites and seasonal craft fairs. By writing a business plan and creating a marketing strategy, however small, you may be eligible to start a small business and deduct the out-of-pocket costs of your hobby on your tax returns.

Saving on Taxes While Seeing the World

You are already deducting your business travel expenses, but you may be missing out on a chance to save even more. It is becoming quite common to combine business travel with leisure trips to bring down the costs of both. For example, if you attend a conference in an exotic location, your travel expenses are likely to be deductible. You can increase your savings by inviting your family along and extending the trip a few days. Their travel won't be tax deductible, and the extra non-working days you take can't be deducted either. However, when costs are allocated appropriately, the total out-of-pocket cost of your family vacation will be substantially lower.

When you use this method of combining business and personal travel, make sure your record-keeping is flawless. Clearly spell out which expenses and activities are work-related versus personal, and keep all relevant documentation including receipts, itineraries, and similar. Your Certified Tax Coach is an important partner for this strategy, ensuring that the business deductions you claim accurately reflect your travel.

Identifying and applying all possible deductions is a bit like searching for sunken treasure. Many potential savings opportunities are well hidden. However, when you put the time and energy into locating the treasure, the financial rewards are well worth your efforts.

ABOUT THE AUTHOR

Luke Gheen, MBA, CPA, CTC

Luke is a longtime resident of Colorado with extensive corporate finance and accounting experience. He graduated with a bachelor's degree in Business Administration from the University of Colorado in 1999, and received his MBA from the University of Colorado in 2007.

Luke started Gheen & Co., CPA in 2010 to help business owners simplify their accounting, save substantial money in tax, and grow their wealth long-term. Since then, Gheen & Co., CPA has become a cutting-edge leader in the tax and accounting industry. They are sought after by business owners all over the country for their emphasis on advanced tax planning, and for ongoing services that help their clients simplify, save, and grow. Their cloud-based client service system has become extremely popular and a model for other firms.

Luke is a member of the American Institute of Certified Public Accountants. He is an avid rower, enjoys reading, and regularly travels to the Finger Lakes region of upstate New York. He relishes spending time with his wife, three sons, daughter, and extended family.

Luke Gheen, MBA, CPA, CTC

Gheen & Co., CPA, LLC

📞 719-785-4864

📍 5030 Boardwalk Dr Ste 250, Colorado Springs, CO, 80919

🌐 www.cpataxcoach.com

✉ cpa@cpataxcoach.com

CHAPTER 6

Bringing Family Members On-Board: How Employing Your Dependents Can Reduce Your Tax Bill

AMY FISCHER, EA, LTC, CTC

You already know that the first step in creating a comprehensive financial strategy is setting goals. As you can imagine, investment advisors and Certified Tax Coaches have heard just about everything from their clients, from plans to visit every country in the world to buying and operating an emu farm.

While some people's financial aspirations fall on the unusual side, most are far more traditional. There is one theme that comes up again and again. A vast majority of clients are focused on a single goal: to build wealth and save on taxes to ensure they can care for their families. They want the security of a steady income, a comfortable home, and the ability to afford quality education for their children.

All of the techniques designed to minimize tax liability can contribute to these family-centric financial objectives. However, what many clients don't realize is that there are extra opportunities to save on taxes when family members are included in the plan. Employing your children can reduce your tax bill while helping them build their own financial planning skills along the way.

There are plenty of benefits to bringing your kids on board as employees, but you have to avoid certain dangers for this technique to be successful. Your Certified Tax Coach has the experience and expertise necessary to ensure that you and your family stay safe during this adventure.

The Benefits of Kids as Employees

Financial literacy is one of the most valuable skills you can teach your kids, and they are never too young to start. Many parents use a system of chores and allowance to illustrate the value of money and offer an opportunity to practice money management and budgeting. However, it is possible to take your lessons a step further in a way that benefits both your children and your bottom-line tax bill.

Hiring your kids to work in your family business comes with a host of advantages. Children learn skills that will serve them throughout their careers, such as the importance of being on time, the nuances of successful customer interactions, and the satisfaction of a job well done. Better still, they might discover a passion for the family business, which simplifies succession planning. In addition, there are substantial financial benefits for your business and personal tax returns. Your tax deductions increase, and some of your income is transitioned to a lower tax bracket. Of course, there are strict IRS requirements that you must meet to qualify for these tax breaks, so be sure to discuss your plan with your Certified Tax Coach before moving forward.

Small Employees Mean Big Tax Savings

As you know, wages and benefits paid to your employees are a deductible expense. The wages you pay your children are no different. You can deduct this amount from your business income to lower your tax bill as you would with any other employee. Some parents save twice by trading in the weekly allowance they give their children for a paycheck from the business. Instead of handing over after-tax dollars, kids are paid with pre-tax funds from the business budget for the business-related work they do.

When calculating the total savings that your business could realize from employing your children, don't forget that you may be able to avoid certain employment taxes. For example, if your business is a sole proprietorship, or you and your spouse are the only partners in a partnership, you do not have to pay the Federal Unemployment Tax Act (FUTA) tax if your child is under the age of 21. If your child is under the age of 18, you can also avoid Social Security and Medicare taxes. However, if anyone other than you and your spouse has an ownership stake in the business or if the business is incorporated, you must pay Social Security, Medicare, and unemployment taxes for your children.

In addition to saving on taxes by paying children with pre-tax dollars, you and your children will realize tax benefits when taxes are filed. If their total income falls below the standard individual deduction, they don't have to pay taxes on their wages at all.

As a result of the 2017 tax code changes, the standard individual deduction increased to $12,000 per person per year as of 2018. That means children can earn up to $12,000 completely tax-free. If their total income is higher than the standard individual deduction, they are still likely to fall into a much lower tax bracket than you do. That means you save money on your income taxes, because you are no longer responsible for taxes on those funds.

Keep in mind that the tax savings techniques you use to reduce your own taxable income can be helpful for your children as well. For example, if your child earns $13,000 in a year, the extra $1,000 can fund an Individual Retirement Account (IRA) in your child's name, and he or she can enjoy all of the associated tax advantages.

Depending on their age and level of skill, your children may be able to earn enough through their work at the family business to cover expenses like clothing and entertainment. They may even be able to contribute to larger expenses like private school tuition, which means you no longer have to pay those bills out-of-pocket with after-tax dollars. Instead, your kids can handle their day-to-day expenditures independently with funds that are minimally taxed or not taxed at all.

Consider this example:

One family was paying $8,000 per year for their son's private school tuition. After consulting with their Certified Tax Coach, they determined that they could realize substantial tax savings by hiring their son as an employee of their small business for eight hours a week. Their son was responsible for basic office duties, such as answering the phone and managing certain paperwork. He was paid $15 an hour for his services, a total of approximately $6,240 per year.

Each week, their son's paycheck was deposited into his individual account, and the school took an automatic withdrawal for a portion of the tuition from that account every month. Since their son's income was below the standard individual deduction, he owed no taxes on his earnings. Meanwhile, the parents were able to avoid taxes on that amount. The overall reduction in taxes made a big difference for the family, offsetting much of the expense associated with attending a private school.

Understanding the "Kiddie Tax"

You have probably heard of the "Kiddie Tax," which is more formally known as the Tax on a Child's Investment and Other Unearned Income. This establishes that children who have income of more than $2,100 may be subject to the same tax rate as their parents. Fortunately, when your children are employees of your business, this tax regulation does not apply. The Kiddie Tax is only assessed on unearned income like interest, dividends, and capital gains distributions.

For your reference, this tax requirement applies to full-time students under the age of 24, as long as parents still provide more than 50 percent of their financial support. Otherwise, once children are over the age of 18, not full-time students, and supporting themselves, they are taxed at the rate appropriate for their level of income.

Popular Ways to Involve Children in the Family Business

Many children enjoy working with their parents. They like spending time together and they enjoy being given responsibility. Best of all, kids like to earn their own money so that they can make some of their own financial decisions.

Before you decide that your child is too young to make a meaningful contribution to your business, take a hard look at the day-to-day tasks that you and your staff members spend time completing. Chances are, an assortment of basic responsibilities can be delegated to your children if you are willing to provide a bit of training. These are some of the most popular ways families get kids involved in the business:

- Addressing envelopes
- Filing documents
- Sorting mail
- Answering phones
- Mowing lawns
- Printing and mailing paperwork
- Cleaning
- Painting
- Modeling for company marketing materials
- Managing social media accounts
- Customer service
- Data entry
- Operating a register
- Bussing tables

Once you have determined which tasks your children will be responsible for, write a job description for the position as you would for any other open position. As children grow older and develop additional skills, you can add additional responsibilities, along with a raise in pay if appropriate. Just be sure to update the job description as needed.

Pitfalls to Avoid When Employing Your Children

Before making your children official employees of your business, there are some important points to consider. As with any tax strategy that lowers your bill, you can expect scrutiny from the IRS, so you want to be sure you have met all necessary requirements. In addition, there are federal and state laws that place restrictions on employment of minors, even if they are family members.

Begin by reviewing the employment laws in your state for minors. The good news is that most do not apply when children are employed by their parents. For example, you probably don't have to worry about age requirements and regulations related to minimum wage. However, your children may be restricted as far as the number of hours they can work in a day or week, and they may not be permitted to work during school hours or late at night.

Federal law prohibits underage workers from certain hazardous tasks and occupations, no matter who employs them. Examples include jobs that rely on machinery to process and package meat products, jobs that require employees to perform work on a scaffold, and tasks that require employees to spend time on a roof. If your business performs hazardous work, ensure that your children are limited to tasks that meet safety regulations such as cleaning, customer service, and office work.

Next, give careful consideration to the specific job and rate of pay you plan to offer your child. If you are ever audited, the IRS will be asking the questions below.

Does the job match business needs?

You are only eligible for writeoffs if you are paying your children to do legitimate work that contributes to business operations. Keep in mind that completing standard household chores does not qualify your child as an employee.

Does the job match the child's age, experience, and skills?

Your teenager may be a financial whiz, but the fact is that you cannot hire a 14-year-old as a "budgeting consultant" or "assistant accountant." Auditors will look for signs that you are trying to decrease your tax rate by exaggerating your child's job responsibilities.

Does the rate of pay match the job responsibilities?

Once you have selected a job for your child that matches his or her level of skill, make sure that the hourly rate is reasonable compared to the pay others receive for similar work. If your child's salary as a part-time receptionist is higher than the amount you pay licensed professionals, you will be sure to attract unwelcome attention from the IRS. If you are not sure how much to pay, survey some of the local temp agencies. You can inquire about the going rate for unskilled labor to ensure that you are paying a reasonable hourly wage.

Make sure that you are fully prepared to answer auditors' questions by keeping careful documentation of your children's work. Insist on complete, accurate timesheets every week, and take note of the tasks that were completed during the hours worked. Both you and your children should sign the timesheets each week to certify that they are correct.

Pay your kids on the same schedule and through the same process that you pay other employees. Direct deposit to an account that is individually owned by your child is always the best option, though this can be a custodial account if appropriate. You can also deposit wages into an IRA account or a Section 529 savings account established to pay for higher education expenses. Finally, make sure to complete the same tax paperwork you would for any other employee. Your children need to have W-4s and I-9s on file, and you must complete W-2s for them each year.

Other Benefits You Can Offer Your Children

The hourly rate you pay your children offers an opportunity to save on taxes, but this isn't the only option for reducing your total tax bill.

Consider offering other employee benefits to increase your total savings. For example, if you are responsible for your children's education expenses, you may wish to set up a tuition reimbursement program. Once you have confirmed that your business is eligible for this type of benefit, you can enjoy substantial savings on the taxes you would otherwise pay for education expenses funded with after-tax dollars.

Another popular option for saving money on taxes is setting up a Section 105 Medical Expense Reimbursement Account (MERP). This benefit is an alternative to traditional health insurance. Businesses use the plan to reimburse employees for their actual medical expenses, including premiums paid for health insurance and out-of-pocket medical expenses. Chances are, you are already paying these bills for your children using after-tax dollars. If your business qualifies for the MERP program, the expenses become writeoffs for your business.

Talk with your Certified Tax Coach about other opportunities to save on taxes by offering tax-deductible benefits to your employees.

Bringing Other Family Members on Board

Though some of the tax saving opportunities that apply to your children don't extend to other family members, hiring any of your dependents can offer tax advantages. This includes your spouse, grandchildren, nieces and nephews, parents, and siblings. Just keep in mind that if any family members other than your own children are minors, they may be subject to the standard employment laws that apply to all children in your state, including minimum wage, age limits, and schedule restrictions.

The Benefits of Employing Your Adult Children

Hiring your adult children may not offer the types of tax breaks you enjoy when your dependent children work for you, but there are other benefits to this arrangement that are worth considering. One of the biggest is that wages you pay your adult children, like the wages you pay any other employee, are writeoffs for your business. If you are in the habit of giving your children cash gifts to keep them afloat during difficult financial times, this is a good way to turn those gifts into tax savings.

Aside from the financial benefits, working for your family business can be an important stepping stone for your adult child's career. As you know, many job postings list experience requirements, even for entry-level positions. The skills and work history your children develop through your family business can enhance their appeal to prospective employers. This same principle applies for children who are unemployed due to layoffs or other work-related issues. Working for the family business prevents resume gaps that must be explained away during the interview process.

Transferring Ownership of the Family Business to Your Children

After years of working alongside you, your children will have a better understanding of the responsibilities involved in owning and operating the family business. More important, they will be able to make a thoughtful decision about whether they want to pursue this option as a career. If your children choose to stick with your family business and they have demonstrated that they have the skills necessary to be successful, you can breathe a sigh of relief. You no longer have to worry about what will happen to your business when you are ready to move on.

The process of transferring ownership of your business to your children may not be as complex as selling to a third party, but there are still a number of details to consider. After all, you want the transition to go smoothly, and you don't want to pay any more taxes than absolutely necessary. Many families choose to make the transition in stages. Children are given partial ownership or shares early in their careers, and additional ownership interests or shares are transferred over time.

There are tax benefits to giving your adult children partial ownership of the business early on. If your business is a partnership, an LLC, or an S-Corporation, you have what is known as a "pass-through" entity. That means that profits and losses realized by the business "pass-through" to the business owners, and each owner pays taxes on his or her share based on individual tax rates. If your child's tax rate is lower than your own, this can mean substantial tax savings for your family.

The Bottom Line

Adding minor children to your payroll can lead to thousands of dollars in tax savings. Your business is able to deduct the wages, and your child can take responsibility for some of the daily expenses that you have been paying with after-tax dollars. Better yet, working for your business allows children to develop critical real-world skills and experience. The lessons they learn about the benefits of hard work and the importance of budgeting can last a lifetime.

The most important thing to remember when you bring your children on board as employees is that the IRS expects them to be doing real work at a reasonable hourly rate. Carefully document your child's responsibilities and ensure that they are necessary for business operations. Pay should be determined by the type of work being done and your child's skills, as well as the amount other workers are paid for similar activities.

Hiring adult children and other family members can also benefit your business. You can enjoy tax savings when you hire anyone who depends on you for financial support, and you can save on income taxes when you transfer partial ownership of the business to those in lower tax brackets. Your Certified Tax Coach is an important partner when it comes to hiring family members. These professionals can help you strike a balance between maximizing your tax savings and minimizing your risk of unwanted attention from the IRS.

ABOUT THE AUTHOR

Amy Fischer, EA, LTC, CTC

Amy is the owner and founder of Expert Business Support, Inc. She operates three offices, two on the West coast (Idaho and Oregon) and one on the East coast (Connecticut). She enjoys serving business owners throughout the country in tax strategy and compliance work.

Amy and her team focus on tax reduction strategies and proactive tax planning concepts. They believe that, with planning for the future, business owners can thrive to new levels and grow and develop as they desire, reducing their tax liabilities with advanced tax planning strategies.

Amy has been preparing taxes and has worked as a tax accountant since early 2000. She started at her father's firm in Idaho, quickly earning a partnership with him, and then successfully running the Idaho office. In 2009 she moved to Oregon to start earning her degree in Sign Language Interpreting. She earned her BA from William Woods University in Fulton, Missouri. During her college years, she secured her license as a tax preparer (LTP) in Oregon, and, shortly thereafter, became an Enrolled Agent (EA), licensed to practice before the Internal Revenue Service. After receiving her EA license, she became a Licensed Tax Consultant (LTC) in Oregon.

Amy actively participates in the company and enjoys the "tax puzzles" that are presented to fit the correct concepts into the desires and needs of each client. She also loves to travel and spend time with her family. She has two children, one boy and one girl. She is fluent in American Sign Language and enjoys learning about other cultures as well as new languages.

Amy Fischer, EA, LTC, CTC

Expert Business Support, Inc.

📞 503-716-8389

📍 PO Box 271356 West Hartford, CT 06127

🌐 expertbusinesssupport.com

✉ aehtax@gmail.com

CHAPTER 7

Minimizing Exposure: Tips for Service Professionals

TINA PITTMAN, CPA, CTC, MBA, CGMA

The work that goes into professional licensing pays off handsomely. Whether you have chosen a career in the financial industry, healthcare, home maintenance, or something else, you have a wide array of options when it comes to putting your skills to work.

As a service professional, you have special opportunities to save on taxes as well. This is especially true if you have your own firm, agency, or private practice. Because your skills are critical for the health and well-being of your community, the tax code is designed to help you thrive. That means you can deduct all sorts of professional expenses, from the cost of continuing education to the specialized equipment you need to be successful.

As with any tax minimization plan, putting the law to work for you can be tricky. It may feel like you are drowning in a sea of taxes at times, but you can save yourself if you allow someone else to help you. Fortunately, your Certified Tax Coach has the experience needed to get you every available deduction so you can maximize your savings. These experts are your lifeguards when it comes to keeping taxes low.

Surround Yourself with Expert Advisors

Although you might be tempted to take a do-it-yourself approach to taxes, standard tax planning software and online tax preparation services aren't enough. These products are designed for the average taxpayer, so the most you can expect is average savings. They use a one-size-fits-all method that is far too broad for the complex needs of a service professional. True tax minimization requires a specialized skill set and customized financial advice that is designed to fit your unique situation.

The first step in your tax minimization plan is to build a knowledgeable financial advisory team. This will ensure that you enjoy all of the deductions and tax savings you are entitled to without taking your focus from your practice. At a minimum, you need a skilled accountant and a Certified Tax Coach who has worked with service professionals before. Your advisors should already have experience with the issues you face, such as student loan debt, continuing education expenses, and the costs associated with the equipment you use in the course of your work.

Consider adding a retirement planning specialist to offer guidance on the particular challenges service professionals face. You may also wish to enlist the skills of a debt specialist who understands the obstacles presented by outstanding student loans. These areas are of critical importance to your financial future, and they are especially difficult to manage when you operate a professional practice.

Once you have assembled a group of skilled financial advisors, be sure to make the most of the services available to you. Instead of an annual meeting, schedule regular check-ins with your advisory team. Frequent meetings give you an opportunity to stay on top of changes in your personal or professional life, so that you can keep your tax minimization strategy on track.

Remember, your Certified Tax Coach offers more than simple tax advice. For instance, he or she can suggest the best timing for major purchases and the best method for incurring expenses to maximize your tax savings opportunities. As you know, there are endless nuances to the tax code, and a slight change in how expenses are recorded can make a big difference. However, this advice is only useful if you get it before you make the purchase or pay the expense.

Your financial advisory team is an important resource to ensure your financial health, both short-term and long-term, but keep in mind that final decisions about your financial affairs belong to you. While you can rely on advisors' experience and expertise when making financial decisions, in the end you must be confident that you have set a course to achieve the financial goals that are important to you. More important, you must be comfortable with the balance of risk and reward you have selected to achieve those goals.

The bottom line is that you will benefit by keeping the lines of communication open with your financial advisors. Arrange regular in-person meetings when possible and schedule video or phone conferences the rest of the time. Keep your financial advisors updated on your financial affairs and request that they ensure you stay informed of any changes in tax regulations that impact you.

Prioritize Retirement Savings

Although your primary goal might be saving on taxes, the good news is that saving for retirement goes hand-in-hand with tax minimization. Lawmakers are committed to making it easier and more affordable to set funds aside for retirement expenses, so many retirement savings programs come with substantial tax advantages.

The best financial move you can make is to contribute the maximum allowable amount to your retirement accounts every year. First, the longer your money stays in your investment accounts, the more it grows. The time value of money cannot be overstated. Second, every penny you put away in a qualified retirement program comes with tax savings. You can make contributions either with pre-tax dollars and pay taxes later when your tax rate is likely to be lower, or you can make contributions with after-tax dollars and enjoy tax-free earnings on those funds.

If you are like most service professionals, setting large amounts aside for retirement is easier said than done at the beginning of your career. Starting your own practice, firm, or agency is an expensive endeavor, and it can take a while for your business to get off the ground. When you also have student loan payments to manage, juggling all of the balls can be a bit overwhelming.

Don't be discouraged if you can't contribute the full amount to your retirement accounts right away. It is common to start with smaller deposits that grow as your business grows. Just be sure that your retirement savings has a priority position in your budget and make it a point to increase your total contributions every year until you reach the maximum.

Don't Focus on Timing the Market

As soon as you expand your portfolio beyond standard banking products like checking and savings accounts, money market programs, and certificates of deposit, you are sure to hear one piece of advice over and over: buy your investments when their value is low and sell when their value is high.

Of course, knowing when the market is at its lowest point and when it is at its peak is the million dollar question, and thousands of financial analysts devote their entire careers to predicting the best times to buy and sell assets. The truth is that it is impossible to time the market with any degree of certainty, though analysts make educated guesses based on the cyclical nature of financial markets, changes in the political climate, and trends in consumer behavior.

Since your attention is devoted to your professional practice, timing the market isn't a practical investment strategy. Instead, you can grow your savings based on the fact that, historically, certain investments reliably increase in value over time. Make regular contributions to your accounts without getting caught up in market hype, and you can generally expect the value of your portfolio to grow.

Invest in Assets that Offer Tax Advantages

There is almost no limit to the industries and assets that offer investment opportunities. If you want to put your money into space travel, worm farming, or comic books, you can certainly do so. There are also more traditional options that cater to specific interests, like mutual funds focused on green energy initiatives or funds that invest in emerging economies. However, when it comes to long-term financial security, the bulk of your funds should be directed towards reliable moneymakers. Better still, you can choose assets that have intrinsic tax benefits, so that you can minimize the taxes you pay when your investments grow.

Mutual funds offer a helpful snapshot of the tax implications of various asset classes. For example, some focus on creating regular income for shareholders. They maximize dividend opportunities, which are taxed at the capital gains rate. Some investors find that such funds aren't a good option because the extra income pushes them into a higher tax bracket. Instead, they choose mutual funds that focus on longer-term capital gains to keep current taxes low. Alternatively, they invest in tax-free government bonds to eliminate most taxes altogether.

If your goal is to minimize your taxes, assets that pay interest and dividends could derail your strategy. Instead, a buy-and-hold plan offers more opportunity to save on taxes, because you can wait to sell your investments until the timing is most beneficial to you for tax purposes. Consult your financial advisors and reliable resources like The Wall Street Journal, SmartMoney, Kiplinger's Personal Finance, and Morningstar for more information on specific investments.

Concentrate on Record-Keeping

By its very nature, your career as a provider of professional services requires meticulous recordkeeping. In healthcare, patients rely on the records you maintain to make medical decisions, and financial services providers hold critical information that can dramatically affect their clients' financial futures. For example, credit decisions are made based on financial records.

Creating and maintaining your own records for all of your financial affairs is equally important for your financial future. The details you log now can translate into thousands of dollars in tax savings when you file your returns. After all, no one can remember every expense incurred over the course of a year without a collection of notes and receipts. More important, these records are your best defense in case of an IRS audit.

It is also worth noting that tax regulations can change over the course of the year, and expenses that weren't deductible when you made the purchase may be deductible by the time you file. One of the most memorable examples of such an instance occurred when the 2003 Tax Act was passed. This law adjusted the bonus depreciation for qualified property from 30 percent to 50 percent, but the change only applied to property acquired between May 5, 2003, and January 1, 2005. Without clear records, it is difficult to prove exactly when a purchase was made, which can threaten your ability to benefit from changes in tax regulation.

The importance of carefully maintained financial records extends beyond your current year's tax return. The IRS can require you to verify the information in your returns going back up to seven years. Simply providing historical tax forms isn't enough. You may need receipts, notes, and minutes from meetings to validate that your previous returns were complete and accurate. Additionally, the notes you keep can help to jog your memory, so you can provide thorough answers to any questions the IRS asks you.

Remember, if you cannot prove that the information on your tax returns is accurate, the financial ramifications are much larger than a revised tax bill. In addition to back taxes, it is likely that you will also be responsible for fees, penalties, and interest.

Create a system for filing receipts and organizing your notes. There are a number of helpful digital services and apps that make this process fast and efficient, eliminating the need to keep hard copies of your receipts. You may wish to ask your Certified Tax Coach for a software recommendation, as working together will be much easier if you both use the same program.

When documenting expenses include the date, time, and place of your purchases, as well as the amount you spent. Add a brief explanation of the business purpose of the expense so you won't have trouble finding the information if you are ever asked. Keep in mind that you can use the same technology you rely on for your professional recordkeeping to simplify your financial recordkeeping. For example, the voice recorder you may use to dictate patient notes is an excellent tool for documenting business expenses.

Select the Right Structure for Your Business

Your choice of business entity can have significant repercussions on your tax bill for the entire time that you are in practice. Believe it or not, your long-term profits may depend as much on how you structure your business as the number of patients or clients you see. There are substantial differences in how you are taxed depending on whether you establish a sole proprietorship, a partnership, a corporation, or a limited liability company (LLC). There are pros and cons of each.

Sole Proprietorships

This option gives you complete control over business decisions, which is a definite plus. However, you also take on all of the company's legal and financial liability. In terms of taxes, it is important to be aware that as a sole proprietorship you could be taxed twice, because your business income is reported through your personal tax returns. In addition to paying income tax, you could be responsible for self-employment taxes as well.

There is another complication to consider. Typically, estimated taxes are not withheld over the course of the year, and unless you take action, nothing is paid to the IRS on your behalf. That means you could be responsible for a large tax bill when you file your returns.

Partnerships

When you build your practice with one or more partners, you face similar tax ramifications to those of a sole proprietorship. Income is divided according to your partnership agreement, and your portion is reported through your personal returns. This business entity is also subject to self-employment taxes.

Business decisions are made according to the partnership agreement, which in most cases requires consensus or compromise between all of the company's owners. Liability is spread among the partners as well, so you could be liable for debts incurred by one of your partners.

Limited Liability Companies (LLCs)

Many professional service providers choose to build their practice as an LLC. As the name suggests, this option reduces legal and financial liability for business owners. While it doesn't completely eliminate your responsibility as a corporation would, an LLC is less expensive to create and administer than a full-fledged corporation. LLCs are subject to many of the same tax expenses that are associated with sole proprietorships and partnerships, including the self-employment tax.

Corporations

It is becoming quite common for professional service providers to incorporate, and the S-Corporation is the most popular option. This type of business entity offers the most protection against personal legal and financial liability for business-related issues. S-Corporation earnings are not subject to self-employment tax, which can mean substantial savings when you file your returns. However, they are costlier to implement and administer than the other three options.

The 2017 Tax Cuts and Jobs Act (TCJA) made dramatic changes to the tax code, and some of the ramifications are still unclear. How the new tax law will impact professional service providers remains to be seen, but for the moment, it does not appear that there will be significant benefits for businesses set up under the aforementioned structures.

The biggest savings are for businesses set up as C-Corporations, which are now subject to a flat tax of just 21 percent. As the tax reform regulations go into effect, it is possible that your Certified Tax Coach will have new recommendations for the structure of your business.

Defer Compensation to Keep Taxes Low

Your income determines which tax rate you pay, and your tax rate is one of the biggest factors in your total tax bill. Essentially, the higher your income, the higher your tax rate, which means greater tax liability. A sudden increase in income, even if it is a one-time event, can be all but lost by the time you pay taxes on those funds.

If you find yourself in this situation, deferring some of your compensation could protect you from an excessive tax bill. By doing this, you basically set aside a portion of the compensation you would normally earn in the current year to be paid at a later point in time.

You can strategically choose the payment date to ensure your tax liability is minimal. For example, income is often deferred until retirement, when most people have lower income and lower tax rates. Since you generally do not pay taxes on the deferred amount until you actually receive it, you can save quite a bit on the total taxes you pay.

Discuss this option with your Certified Tax Coach, especially in light of the tax reform legislation. Deferring income may help certain professionals qualify for a new tax deduction under the revised tax code.

Investigate Exclusive Deductions for Professional Service Providers

There are tax benefits to owning a practice, firm, or agency that you simply can't access if you are employed by others. This is one of the reasons so many professionals prefer self-employment. You can get creative within the confines of the tax code to keep your tax bill as low as possible. For example, you can employ members of your family if you have jobs available that match their abilities. As long as the work is legitimate and age-appropriate, you have an opportunity to realize significant tax savings.

A lesser-known option for reducing your taxes is to create a closely held insurance company. Such a company offers protection if your revenues go down or you become involved in a lawsuit, and you gain a variety of tax advantages along the way.

All of the tactics discussed in this chapter can increase the success of your comprehensive tax minimization strategy, but be sure that you don't neglect to claim the many writeoffs available to you as a professional service provider. In some cases, a small change to your business practices can mean big tax savings as you become eligible for a variety of additional deduction opportunities. Here are a few of the writeoffs that are most often overlooked:

- **Equipment Purchases** – The expensive equipment you use in your practice can often be leased, but many professionals choose to purchase it outright. While you can deduct depreciation expenses for these items, your tax savings may be greater when you lease. This offers you an option to deduct the full expense of the equipment faster than you would through a purchase.

- **Volunteering** – Professional services are in high demand, and often the people who need them most can't afford to pay. You may be helping to fill this gap by volunteering your skills. This is an important way you can give back to your community, and you don't have to take on the full expense alone. You may be able to deduct some of the costs of providing services as a charitable contribution.

- **Staff Benefits** – No matter how successful your practice is, the cost of providing your staff with medical and retirement benefits can seem unaffordable. Fortunately, the tax law is designed to encourage small businesses to offer these opportunities to employees. Before you decide what sort of benefits you will provide, have a look at the tax deductions, reduced rates, and credits available to you.

- **Home Office Expenses** – Most professionals keep a dedicated area of their home for handling business matters, because running a practice is a round-the-clock job. In some cases, professionals practice out of their home offices, seeing patients and clients in rooms set aside for this purpose. If part of your home meets specific criteria for home office expense deductions, you can enjoy substantial tax savings. Work with your Certified Tax Coach to determine whether and how you can create a space that meets eligibility requirements.

If you aren't sure whether you can deduct a business-related expense, go ahead and log it with your other receipts and records. When you are ready to file, your Certified Tax Coach will help you separate items that can be deducted from those that cannot.

State and Local Tax Laws

It is easy to become so focused on minimizing your federal tax bill that you neglect potential savings on your state and municipal tax returns. This is an error that can cost you thousands of dollars. Spend some time learning more about special exemptions and credits that your state and city offer for professional service providers. Some local governments reward you for locating your office in a distressed community, and others offer tax savings when you operate out of a historic building. There are a variety of city and state-specific tactics for reducing your tax bill, and it is worth your while to explore these opportunities.

Your ability to reach financial goals depends, in part, on decisions you make today. Creating and implementing a comprehensive tax minimization strategy is an important component of your long-term wealth. Focus on both your short-term and long-term tactics for saving and investing, and make sure that you keep as much of what you earn as possible by keeping your tax bill as low as possible. Your Certified Tax Coach is an important partner in your success, and you can count on these professionals to keep you afloat in a churning sea of tax regulations.

ABOUT THE AUTHOR

Tina Pittman, CPA, CTC, MBA, CGMA

Tina Pittman is a founding member of Your Accountant, LLC, specializing in proactive tax planning, accounting, and business consulting services for service professionals and manufacturing entrepreneurs. She is the author of *Straight Talk About Small Business Success in PA*. She is a CTC and is licensed as a CPA in Pennsylvania. Tina also received her designation as a Certified Global Management Accountant from the AICPA and an MBA degree from Campbell University.

Tina is a member of AICPA, PICPA, and NATP. She received an award for Excellence in Service to the Medical Community in 2011.

Tina has more than 30 years' experience in tax planning and preparation, accounting, and business consulting. She started her career when she was inspired by her husband, who opened his own small business. With her education and business experience, Tina is in a perfect position to help small business entrepreneurs with profitability and reduction of tax liability. Over the years, she has seen many small businesses struggle due to high tax burdens. She is an expert in resolving tax burdens, putting thousands of tax dollars back into the entrepreneur's pocket. Tina is well known as a proactive tax planner among her peers; in addition to her primary business, she educates tax preparers in providing value added services.

Tina believes in serving the community and will continue to give back. She currently sits on the PA-NATP Board of Directors. She is a former Board Member for Chambersburg Boys & Girls Club and Treasurer for a local church.

You may schedule your free discovery session at www.calendly.com/tinapittman.

Tina Pittman, CPA, CTC, MBA, CGMA

Your Accountant, LLC

📞 (717) 504-8808

📍 947 Wayne Avenue PMB 229 Chambersburg, PA 17201

🌐 www.pittman-cpa.com
www.innovativetaxplanning.com

✉️ tina@pittman-cpa.com

CHAPTER 8

Treading Water in a Flood of Medical Expenses

WILLIAM STUKEY, CPA, CTC

The cost of healthcare is rising rapidly. Out-of-pocket expenses for individuals and families went up 66 percent in the ten-year period from 2005–2015. This is double the rate that wages grew in the same period, which means a flood of financial pressure for US households. Unfortunately, the upward trend in medical expenses continues.

In the United States, the total bill for healthcare rose from just 5 percent of the economy in 1960 to 17.9 percent of the economy in 2016. Projections indicate that this figure could be as high as 19.9 percent by 2025. This includes spending by individuals, private sector businesses, state governments, and the federal government.

In dollars, the totals are astonishing. The tab for 2016 was approximately $3.3 trillion, which is an average of $10,348 per person. Of that amount, $665 billion came from private sector employers, mostly to subsidize health insurance premiums for employees. These subsidies cover about 75 percent of employees' premiums, which is a significant benefit. In the past five years, premiums have increased an average of 19 percent, and they are still going up. Individual health insurance plans cost approximately $7,000 in 2017, and family plans were as high as $19,000.

With healthcare expenses flooding homes and businesses, it is easy to get sucked under. A shocking number of families and businesses have lost everything to medical bills. Fortunately, there are a variety of provisions in the tax code to reduce the financial burden for employers and employees, but only if you know how to apply them to your advantage.

A Medical Expense Reimbursement Plan (MERP), also referred to as a Section 105 plan, can be the lifeboat your business needs to survive the high cost of employee healthcare. If you cannot participate in a MERP, you may be eligible for a Health Savings Account (HSA).

Both products offer tax savings for those who need to be rescued from their steep medical bills. Your Certified Tax Coach can help you employ these life boats as part of your comprehensive tax minimization strategy.

The Downside of Itemizing Medical Expenses

Since MERPs and HSAs are not well understood by a majority of taxpayers, most try to save money by itemizing medical deductions. However, this method is rarely the best option for minimizing your tax bill.

The biggest disadvantage of itemizing deductions is the high expense threshold you must meet before realizing savings. In recent years, the tax code only permitted deductions for medical expenses exceeding 10 percent of your Adjusted Gross Income. For example, if your Adjusted Gross Income was $100,000 and you incurred $12,000 in out-of-pocket medical expenses, you might see tax savings on the last $2,000 in costs.

Reaching the 10 percent threshold puts a heavy financial burden on average households. Most don't meet the requirement unless there was a serious illness or medical emergency during the year. As a result, they don't enjoy any tax savings on medical expenses. MERP and HSA plans don't have this drawback, which creates more opportunity for taxpayers to save on medical expenses.

The Basics of a Medical Expense Reimbursement Plan (MERP)

The cost of providing health benefits for employees is an ongoing challenge for businesses. Even the largest organizations struggle to manage these expenses. However, eliminating medical benefits isn't a viable option in most cases. Top talent is hard to come by, especially when unemployment rates are low. Attracting and retaining high-quality employees requires caring for their health and well-being through medical coverage.

Implementing a MERP offers an opportunity to reduce costs associated with employee healthcare by minimizing taxes on these expenses. In essence, the MERP is a tax-advantaged fund that the business owns and manages. The company contributes to the account, and when employees incur medical expenses, they are reimbursed through the MERP. Every penny that the business contributes to a MERP plan is tax-free.

Employee health insurance premiums have always been paid with pre-tax dollars, but most other medical expenses do not offer the same savings. The most important advantage of a MERP versus traditional methods of managing employee healthcare costs is that you can pay for additional types of medical expenses with pre-tax dollars. Examples of expenses that can be reimbursed include health insurance premiums, deductibles, and co-insurance.

Businesses save on income taxes at the federal and state levels in addition to saving money on payroll taxes. Employers have flexibility in the criteria used to determine which staff members are included in the plan. Funds in a MERP can be used to pay the healthcare costs for entire families, adding the flexibility you and your employees need to bring out-of-pocket expenses down.

Expenses paid through a MERP are not subject to the same limits as medical deductions on a tax return. When employees participate in a MERP, there is no need to itemize medical deductions and no individual income requirement. Up to 100 percent of expenses can be covered through the fund, and there is no bottom or cap unless the business sets one. This offers businesses an opportunity to save on expenses associated with employee healthcare, because you can create a plan that reimburses expenses up to a set amount for each covered individual.

Businesses are not subject to mandatory contributions, since MERP dollars are specifically earmarked for medical bills. Best of all, unlike other medical spending accounts, there is no requirement to "use it or lose it." Though these plans are available to a wide variety of businesses, they are most valuable for those that are closely held, service-oriented, or staffed primarily with part-time workers.

Acceptable MERP Expenses

As a basic rule, expenses that would otherwise qualify for a medical deduction on tax returns can also be paid through a MERP. Examples of such expenses include the following:

- Medical insurance premiums
- Long-term care insurance premiums
- Medicare and Medigap insurance premiums
- Copayments
- Deductibles
- Prescription costs
- Dental care and orthodontia expenses
- Vision care and LASIK expenses
- Hearing aids
- Chiropractic fees
- Fertility treatment
- Costs associated with schools for the disabled
- Non-prescription medication for which the patient has a prescription
- Mileage and transportation costs associated with obtaining medical care
- Acupuncture

- Cost of modifications made to the home to support a disability
- Long-term care
- Nursing services

Other, less common medical expenses may qualify for MERP coverage if they are prescribed by a physician. For example, some people have received reimbursement for the cost of health club fees when their doctors prescribed a certain type of physical activity to treat a medical condition. MERPs have reimbursed families for the expense of clarinet lessons to treat issues with the teeth and jaw, as well as Tae Kwon Do lessons to manage the symptoms of ADHD.

MERP coverage is limited to employees and eligible family members, so business owners are often excluded from the plan. For example, sole proprietors are not employees of their businesses, so they cannot generally participate. However, spouses or dependents may be eligible if they are bonafide employees of the organization.

Since MERP reimbursements can be used to supplement a spouse's medical insurance, sole proprietors may receive some coverage through their spouse if their spouse is an employee. Full partners are not considered employees for the purpose of MERP, but limited partners and those who own less than five percent of the business do qualify.

Companies that are organized as C-Corporations can leverage a MERP for employee medical expenses. In this situation, company founders may be considered employees of the corporation. As long as they are treated as employees of the business and they are paid a reasonable salary for their contributions, they can receive MERP reimbursements.

This caveat doesn't extend to S-Corporation shareholders who own more than two percent of the business. Though S-Corporations can extend MERP benefits to employees, shareholders are not eligible.

Potential Pitfalls of a MERP

Once you have determined that your business will benefit from implementing a MERP to cover employee medical expenses, make sure that your program design avoids potential pitfalls. Note the three most common issues that face MERP administrators.

Inconsistent Coverage

If your MERP covers one employee, it must cover all eligible employees to qualify for tax savings. This requirement is referred to as non-discrimination. Essentially, you can't pick and choose who will receive benefits based on level of income, performance, or similar. The only employees you can exclude fall into the following categories:

- Individuals under the age of 25
- Employees who work less than 35 hours per week
- Seasonal employees or those who work less than nine months of each year
- Staff members with less than three years of service

Controlled Group Exclusions

Diversification is a good idea in investments and in business. Many companies own a collection of subsidiaries offering a range of products and services. However, despite the fact that each subsidiary is technically a separate company, employees in one group cannot be treated differently than another group. As long as the companies have the same primary owner, all employees must have the same access to MERP benefits.

Affiliated Service Groups

Sometimes, it makes sense for businesses to divide functions into separate entities. For example, a law firm may create an affiliate company to provide administrative and paralegal support to the firm's attorneys. This doesn't mean MERP benefits can be offered to one group and not the other. If a business receives 50 percent or more of its gross income from another organization, the two are considered one company for the purpose of employees' MERP eligibility.

Reimbursing employees for medical expenses through a MERP can dramatically decrease your tax bill. However, this area of the tax code is complicated, and it is easy to run afoul of the laws. Your Certified Tax Coach knows the ins and outs of these regulations, as well as how they should be applied in real-world situations. You can count on these experienced advisors to guide you safely through the design and implementation of your program.

The Basics of a Health Savings Account (HSA)

If you are a business owner who has employees, but your business does not offer a MERP plan or you have employees who do not qualify, there is still an alternative that can help them save on taxes.

A Health Savings Account (HSA) is similar to a MERP, but it is designed for individuals who are responsible for their own medical expenses. HSAs are intended to be used in conjunction with high-deductible medical insurance plans to offset the financial impact of uncovered healthcare expenses.

High-deductible medical insurance is also known as catastrophic coverage. These plans protect your employees from expenses incurred through major medical events like a serious illness or a devastating accident. Qualified employees are expected to pay out-of-pocket for day-to-day costs associated with the basic care they receive throughout the year.

The deductible is much larger through these plans than it is with traditional plans. For tax purposes, a high-deductible plan has a minimum deductible of $1,350 for individuals and $2,700 for families. The maximum out-of-pocket they are expected to pay under these plans is $6,650 for individuals and $13,300 for families. Out-of-pocket expenses include deductibles, copayments, and other health-related expenses, but their premiums are not included in these figures.

If you offer this type of medical insurance, your employees are eligible to open an HSA account. Employers that offer high-deductible medical plans often simplify the process of initiating an HSA by partnering with a provider. In many cases, the company contributes a certain amount to the account each year on the employees' behalf, but the real power of these plans occurs when pre-tax contributions to the HSA are made by the employees.

Keep in mind that there are limits to the amount that can be contributed each year. In 2018, the cap is $3,450 for individuals and $6,900 for families. This represents an increase of $50 per year for individuals and $150 for families as compared to 2017 figures. If the recipient is age 55 or older, additional catch-up contribution of up to $1,000 annually can be made.

The funds deposited are deducted from the employees' paychecks before taxes. When they incur a covered expense, they pay the bill and submit a form to the plan administrator for reimbursement. In many cases, a debit card is provided that can be used to pay eligible expenses directly from the HSA.

Funds deposited in the HSA are available forever. If the money is not used, it accrues interest. Over time, some people accumulate a substantial amount that they can invest in a variety of assets to increase earnings. Accounts are portable, so they follow employees all the way through retirement, even though they may change employers. If they are ever ineligible for the plan, they can still keep the same account. They simply cannot make additional pre-tax contributions until regaining eligibility.

Employees are eligible for an HSA if they are covered by a high-deductible medical insurance plan and are not entitled to Medicare. However, they cannot open this type of account if someone else is able to claim them as a dependent.

Employees are not the only people eligible for HSAs; corporate owners, partners, and the self-employed are eligible as well.

The expenses that can be reimbursed through an HSA are identical to those listed under the MERP program. In addition, the HSA funds can be used to pay for COBRA premiums if such coverage becomes necessary. If HSA funds are withdrawn for a purpose that does not qualify under HSA guidelines, the account holder will be responsible for income taxes on the amount distributed. If the distribution takes place before the age of 65, there may also be a 20 percent tax penalty.

The biggest impact HSAs have on tax bills is that contributions are made pre-tax, even if deductions are not itemized. As long as HSA funds are used for qualified health expenses, no tax liability is incurred. Better still, taxes are not assessed on contributions from employers. The funds deposited by employers are not included in taxable income, which means increased compensation without increased tax liability.

Other Ways to Save

Though the MERP and the HSA present two powerful opportunities for tax savings, they aren't the right choice for every individual and business. Sometimes, eligibility restrictions exclude participation, and other times, there are administrative or other obstacles to implementing these plans. In these situations, consider alternative choices to reduce your tax liability for healthcare expenses.

Individuals who purchase health insurance under the Affordable Care Act (ACA) may qualify for tax credits to offset their premium expenses. These credits work a bit differently from other types of tax credits, because they are paid at the beginning of the year to make premiums affordable for low-to-moderate income households. The value of your credit is based on a sliding scale, so that those in lower-income households receive more assistance.

ACA credits are available to households with income of at least 100 percent of the federal poverty line but no more than 400 percent of the federal poverty line. In 2017, the federal poverty line was $12,060 for one person, $16,240 for a family of two, and $24,600 for a family of four.

The government has an interest in encouraging small businesses to offer health benefits to their employees. The primary reason many of these companies don't offer insurance is the high cost of premiums. In response to this concern, there are now an assortment of tax credits available for small businesses that choose to provide employees with coverage.

The Small Business Health Care Tax Credit is designed for the smallest of small businesses: those with 25 full-time employees or less. The average income of each employee must be $50,000 or less, and the business must pay more than 50 percent of employees' medical insurance premiums to qualify. In addition, coverage must be made available to all employees working 30 or more hours per week, though it does not have to be offered for spouses and dependents.

If your business meets all of these criteria, you may qualify for a credit of up to 50 percent of the expenses you incur for employees' premiums. Non-profit organizations that meet these criteria may be eligible for a credit of up to 35 percent of employee premium costs. If you are unable to use your full credit in the current tax year, the remainder can be rolled over to future years.

The seemingly endless rise in healthcare costs creates a significant financial burden for individual taxpayers and for businesses. In some cases, these expenses can pull you under completely. A substantial percentage of personal bankruptcies are driven by massive medical bills. Your Certified Tax Coach is the lifeguard you need to keep from drowning in a sea of healthcare costs.

Individual taxpayers and businesses of every size can benefit from careful planning to minimize taxes on medical expenses. Businesses can lower their tax liability by implementing a Medical Expense Reimbursement Plan, and individuals can realize significant tax savings from a Health Savings Account. When these options aren't available, consider alternative ways to take advantage of deductions and credits to keep your tax bills low.

ABOUT THE AUTHOR

William (Bill) Stukey, CPA, CTC

Bill Stukey is a CPA, CTC and the CEO of Wm Stukey & Associates, LLC ("WSA") which provides virtual accounting, tax and advisory services to dentists and physicians with solo practices and multiple practices in Texas and throughout the United States. Bill is an author and speaker who specializes in the health care industries. His firm also works with other industries that include oil and gas, restaurant chains, technology, entertainment, professional sports, and manufacturing.

There are six CPAs at WSA, most with Big Four experience. The WSA team has tax experience with Fortune 500 companies and international tax experience as well. Our primary focus is advanced tax planning to minimize tax burden. WSA has trained tax strategists on your side of the table working to minimize tax, defer tax, and avoid higher taxes at every opportunity. Bill and his team of CPAs focus on advanced tax planning education seminars and study programs on a weekly basis. WSA uses this experience to minimize income taxes for middle market companies, small business owners, and investors.

Bill has over 24 years of experience in public accounting and was previously CFO of a $400 million financial institution.

One of our many strategies is to put our clients in a tax-free situation fully ready for retirement.

William Stukey, CPA, CTC

Wm Stukey & Associates, LLC

📞 817-481-3265

📍 1705 W Northwest Hwy, Ste 220 Grapevine, Texas 76051

🌐 www.avirtualcpafirm.com

✉ billstukey@avirtualcpafirm.com

CHAPTER 9

The Real Estate Rescue: How Property Protects Your Wealth

DAWN JAMES, CPA, CTC

A quick look at the portfolios of today's most successful investors shows they have something in common. They all rely on real estate in one way or another to protect their wealth against economic ups and downs. Owning property automatically qualifies you for certain tax advantages, and the potential for passive income generation can be a lifesaver when other assets lose value.

As your Certified Tax Coach will tell you, investing in real estate supports a proven three-prong strategy for long-term success.

- Reduce your taxable income, while simultaneously growing sources of untaxed income

- Maximize your use of tax credits and tax deductions to limit your tax liability

- Structure your income in such a way that it qualifies for the lowest possible tax bracket

Real estate is uniquely positioned for building wealth, as lawmakers have consistently chosen to expand opportunities for lowering related taxes. The income you generate from property ownership may, dollar for dollar, do more to increase the value of your portfolio than any other investment you make.

Safe Passage Through the Whirlpool of Real Estate Tax

Of course, if creating wealth through property ownership was simple, everyone would do it. Maximizing the value of real estate investments takes commitment. There are specific parameters to follow when it comes to which real estate you buy, what financing method you use, and how you generate income from the property. When you do it right, the payoff can be substantial.

At the most basic level, real estate is an excellent investment because it builds wealth in two ways. First, while you own the property, you can rent it out for others to use. The resulting income can subsidize your lifestyle or fund other investments, depending on your financial goals. Rental income serves as your long-term life preserver, because you always have the option of keeping your income-generating properties after you retire. If you haven't set aside enough in retirement accounts, real estate assets ensure you can maintain the lifestyle you want.

Second, real estate has a strong historical record of appreciation, and many investors realize substantial gains when they sell. Building wealth through capital gains is particularly lucrative today, in the aftermath of the 2008 recession. In the years preceding the financial crisis, real estate prices had increased dramatically. When the bubble burst, the market crashed. Many investors were unable to weather this storm, and they were forced out of the market.

More than a decade later, demand has not returned to pre-recession levels, which means there is a large inventory of value-priced property. Better still, there is no sign of the intense competition that marked the first few years of the 21st century. Many investors have moved on to other sorts of assets, and far more individuals and families prefer renting to buying.

The Basics of Buying Real Estate

Building wealth through buying real estate relies on specific, proven strategies. The following tactics are most critical to your success.

- Search for properties that you can purchase for less than average prices as compared to similar real estate in the same general location. If you choose to sell in the future, you will almost certainly enjoy a boost in profits.

- Keep the number one real estate industry adage top of mind: location, location, location. Purchase property in the best neighborhood you can afford. A simple drive-by isn't always enough to evaluate the area. Analyze available data such as income levels, zoning, demographics, and rental trends to get a complete picture of the location you are considering for your investment.

- When studying residential properties, pay close attention to neighborhood amenities that your renters will be likely to value. Examples include high quality schools, access to recreation facilities, and proximity to airports, train stations, and major highways. All of these will enable you to generate more rental income.

If you see the perfect investment property for sale, you may have to act fast. Though competition is nothing like the pre-2008 levels, good value often sells quickly. Be sure you are ready to make an offer by consulting with your Certified Tax Coach before you start your search.

Maximizing Income and Minimizing Taxes for Your Rental Property

After the paperwork is signed and the sale has closed, the expertise of a Certified Tax Coach is more helpful than ever. The next step is to ensure you are making the most of your property's potential for rental income while simultaneously keeping tax liability as low as possible. Finding balance takes a certain amount of finesse, but if you get stuck, your Certified Tax Coach can bail you out.

Begin by analyzing the market to gauge the standard rental charges for similar properties. While you want to keep the rent low enough to limit tenant turnover, it must be high enough to cover the expenses associated with owning the building. This includes your mortgage payments, property taxes, and insurance, as well as the maintenance that every structure requires to stay in top condition. If possible, set the rent at a figure that leaves some money left over every month. You can use this extra amount to fund personal expenses or you can reinvest it in other assets.

Before you commit to a traditional landlord/tenant relationship, consider the tax ramifications of passive rental income versus active income. Typically, the rent you receive each month falls in the passive category, which is not necessarily a problem. However, if you have losses on passive income, it cannot be used to offset the tax liability of other income.

If this presents an issue, you may wish to consider alternative rental arrangements that are more likely to qualify as active for tax purposes. Here are a few of the most popular methods of generating active income from real estate.

- Provide "extraordinary" services to long-term tenants, to the extent that they are actually paying for your services and the rental is an afterthought
- Offer short-term rentals of seven days or less, as this transforms your investment from a passive rental to an active lodging business
- Combine short-term rentals of 30 days or less with "significant" services
- Use the property as premises for a business you own

None of these options automatically guarantees that your rental income will be considered active for tax purposes, but they are worth pursuing, as you can realize significant tax savings in certain situations.

The Truth About "Flipping" Real Estate

A number of reality shows centered on "flipping" real estate have gained popularity. As a result, many potential real estate investors believe that building wealth through property ownership involves buying a building, making improvements, and selling it for a profit. While a limited number of home improvement experts do make a living this way, flipping property for profit is unreliable at best.

Those who are most successful at flipping homes already have the skills needed to make renovations or they have a network of contractors that can get the job done for a lower-than-average price. They negotiate the price of their purchase based on the expected cost of repairs, and their profit is the difference between standard repair estimates and the actual cost of the work. Such investments are intended to be short-term, and many such properties are resold in less than a year. This changes how the income is classified for tax purposes.

Many of the tax benefits available to property owners can't be applied to flipped real estate. The relevant tax code is designed to encourage long-term investment. For example, those who buy and sell multiple properties in the same year are considered dealers for tax purposes–not investors. Dealers file taxes as a business, and the profits realized from property sales are treated as business income, not capital gains.

Expand Your Income Through Smart Financing

After looking into all of the steps required to generate rental income, some potential real estate investors are discouraged. The process of identifying and purchasing property then attracting and retaining tenants seems like a lot of work for a relatively small reward. However, the most successful investors don't stop at a single property. By determining the best financing options, they amplify earnings dramatically.

This example shows the standard method of investing in real estate:

> You have $300,000 to invest and you elect to purchase a single property with cash. No financing is required. You determine that you can charge $2,000 per month for rent, $800 of which is earmarked for various expenses like maintenance, taxes, and insurance. Your profit is $1,200 each month. When you choose to sell, the difference between the amount you paid and the sales price puts additional profits in your pocket.

The trick to transforming a single real estate purchase into a large portfolio of assets is simple. This example illustrates how quickly your real estate holdings can grow when you take advantage of financing opportunities:

> With the same $300,000, you purchase three separate properties, all of which are valued at $300,000. This is accomplished with a $100,000 down payment on each, along with $200,000 of financing. You charge $2,000 per month for each rental unit, and your expenses for each unit increase to $1,200 per month. You receive $6,000 in revenue, pay out $3,600 in expenses, and realize a profit of $2,400. As a bonus, all of the properties increase in value during the period you own them. When you sell, you enjoy triple the capital gains.

Finally, owning more properties reduces risk in much the same way as diversifying your investment portfolio. If there is an issue at one location, your income from the other locations gives you a safety net to cover expenses.

Swimming Safely Through a Sea of Tax Regulations

Identifying investment properties, securing financing, and filling rental units with quality tenants is a major undertaking, and you will want to protect every penny of your profits. Your Certified Tax Coach is a lifesaver when it comes to keeping your tax expense low while you build your wealth as a property owner.

A Rising Tide Floats All Boats

The beauty of real estate is that it has an extremely reliable history of appreciating over time. While there can be dips in property values, the market has always recovered eventually, building wealth for property owners. At its most basic, the concept works like this: You purchase real estate valued at $500,000. Five years later, it is valued at $550,000. Your assets have increased by a total of $50,000.

How you manage the wealth created by the appreciation in property values has a direct impact on your tax liability. Here are some options to consider as next steps.

- **Do nothing** – There is no tax liability for the increased value if you do not sell the property.

- **Refinance** – This is another method of using smart financing. Many investors refinance their properties based on the increased value, so they can access the equity they have in the property. The cash can be used to fund personal expenses or it can be reinvested in additional real estate purchases. Either way, accessing your equity through refinancing carries no tax obligations.

- **Sell** – This option gives you an opportunity to access the money you have invested in the property, but there may be significant tax implications. The difference between your original purchase price and the final sale price is considered capital gains, and you are subject to the relevant capital gains taxes. Fortunately, there are ways to chip away at this obligation so that you can keep more of your profits.

- **1031 Exchange** – One of the most effective ways of minimizing your capital gains tax obligations is to reinvest the proceeds of your sale. If you sell one property and purchase another within specified timeframes, your capital gains taxes are deferred.

Keep in mind that capital gains on your primary residence are taxed differently than capital gains on investment properties. You can sell your primary residence once every two years without being assessed taxes on some or all of your capital gains. Individuals are eligible for up to $250,000 in tax-free capital gains, and the amount doubles for married couples. This can make it well worth your while to wait a few months if you plan to relocate but you haven't hit the two year mark.

The Tax Deduction Lifeboat

Every dollar you earn, whether from working or investing, is subject to one or more tax regulations. Keeping more of your income in your pocket requires careful attention to tax savings strategies. The tax code is intended to keep tax rates fair. This is accomplished through a long list of opportunities for deducting portions of your income from the total taxable amount.

Tracking the deductions you are eligible for and providing the necessary documentation to support your eligibility is a big job. However, when it comes to real estate, building your wealth depends on maximizing your deductions. Fortunately, your Certified Tax Coach is ready to assist.

Here are some popular deductions property owners take advantage of.

Repairs and Maintenance

It's true that you have to spend money to make money, and your rental income depends on keeping the property in good condition. The cost of repairs and maintenance often qualify for deduction. Keep in mind that there is a difference between home repairs and home improvements. Repairs keep the existing features of the property in working order so you can continue to earn rental income, while improvements are intended to increase the value of the property. In most cases, home improvements do not qualify for a tax deduction under the tax code.

Consult your tax advisor about the nuances of this distinction, as there are some gray areas. For example, the expense of repairing damaged window frames by returning them to their original state may qualify for deduction, while replacing damaged window frames with new, energy-efficient alternatives may not.

Finally, as with anything related to your taxes, documentation of repair and maintenance costs is critical. Keep your receipts and make sure they are itemized. To the extent possible, request separate invoices for each project you do, so that you don't run into trouble when one is classified as a repair expense and another is classified as an improvement.

Depreciation

Building wealth through real estate investment depends, in part, on appreciation of the property value. However, there is an interesting paradox that will save you money on your taxes. While the overall value of the property appreciates, components of the property depreciate. This includes structures like homes, garages, and buildings. Each year, the IRS permits you to deduct a certain amount of depreciation from your taxable rental income. Generally, commercial buildings are depreciated over 39 years, while residential properties are depreciated over 27.5 years.

It is possible to speed the depreciation process along, so that you can take depreciation deductions in a compressed timeframe. This requires the use of cost segregation, which is a study that catalogs each element of the property and places the components into appropriate depreciation categories.

When you choose cost segregation, calculating depreciation is complex. Different types of improvements depreciate at different rates. In addition, repair expenses must be assigned to the correct area of the property if they are to be included in your depreciation calculation.

Some components that can be depreciated for tax purposes include the following.

- Homes
- Attached structures, such as garages
- Detached structures, such as barns and sheds
- Improvements to the land, for example driveways, paths, and some landscaping
- Critical elements of the building, including cabinets, flooring, and the roof
- Some major appliances, such as the water heater and furnace

When you maximize depreciation deductions on your tax returns, you are able to recover much of the expense that comes with improvements and repairs. If recovering these funds quickly is a priority, consider depreciation rates when making your plans. For example, the amount you invest in new cabinets will be recovered rapidly, while the expense of a new roof may take a bit longer to recoup.

Less Common Tax Credits

If your goal is to maximize your tax credits, talk to your Certified Tax Coach before you buy. Certain types of real estate qualify for special tax consideration. For example, some buildings have historical significance. The tax code offers incentives for those willing to purchase and rehabilitate such properties. Generally, such credits apply to both residential and commercial buildings constructed before 1936. They can also be used for properties that have already received certification as a historical site. You may qualify for credits ranging from 10 percent–20 percent and possibly more if the property is located in a qualified disaster area.

There are also tax credits available for investors who develop affordable housing projects. Rental units must be priced for low-income tenants, and you must agree to rent control regulations in order to qualify. If this type of investment appeals to you, be sure to consult with your real estate attorney and Certified Tax Coach for additional details before you commit.

Advanced Tax Minimization Strategies

Most real estate investors rely on careful use of deductions and credits to keep their tax bills low. A handful take tax savings to the next level with large-scale maneuvers. Here are three advanced approaches.

Self-Directed IRAs

Sophisticated investors know that retirement savings programs offer an excellent opportunity to minimize tax liability. They use the power of tax-advantaged retirement savings programs to shield their earnings from the IRS.

Individual Retirement Accounts (IRAs) are the gold standard when it comes to tax reduction because they are governed by a set of rules specifically designed to keep taxes low. The programs are intended to encourage retirement savings, so earnings enjoy a tax-deferred status. Instead of paying taxes on the income in the year it is earned, taxes are assessed much later, when retirees begin taking distributions from their accounts. For most people, this results in significant tax savings, because after leaving the work force, retirees are in a much lower tax bracket.

You can include a wide range of asset classes in your IRA, from stocks and bonds to real estate holdings. You must meet three criteria to protect your investment income.

- Your IRA must be self-directed. Traditional and Roth IRAs can't invest in property.

- You must appoint a trustee to manage your self-directed IRA. The trustee is responsible for managing income and expenses for your real estate investments.

- Your residence cannot be included in a self-directed IRA, and you can't move property you already own into your retirement account. If you choose to add real estate investments to your self-directed IRA, you must purchase additional property with funds that are already covered by your retirement savings plan.

If you meet these eligibility requirements, the income earned from your real estate investments gets the same favorable tax treatment as the rest of your retirement portfolio. Your taxes are deferred, so your wealth builds faster as the magic of compound interest works for you.

Building a Real Estate Business

Some investors discover they have a gift for identifying properties with significant earning potential. If you are one of them, launching a real estate business offers extraordinary opportunity. These businesses enjoy additional tax benefits on investment properties, because they combine deductions and credits available for real estate with deductions and credits available for businesses.

This particular strategy doesn't apply to companies that buy and sell real estate. It is intended for businesses that purchase and manage a portfolio of investment properties. If you choose this type of business, you could be eligible for any or all of these additional deductions.

- Expenses related to renting your properties, such as advertising, cleaning, and similar
- A portion of the expenses related to your primary residence, for business owners who maintain a home office
- Compensation and benefits paid to your staff members
- Cost of professional services for your business, such as accountants, financial advisors, and attorneys
- Mileage, travel, and lodging expenses related to managing properties owned by your business

With every business deduction you reduce your taxable income, so your bill goes down and your profits go up. Better still, your business transforms real estate income from passive to active, so you can use business losses to offset gains in other areas. Your Certified Tax Coach can provide you with the details you need to maximize this savings opportunity.

Employing Your Family

Your real estate startup already qualifies for a variety of business deductions, and you can amplify your total savings with an additional step. Instead of hiring from the outside to staff your company, employ your family members to manage properties owned by the business. This qualifies you for even more deductions that you wouldn't otherwise be able to access, and your family will benefit, too. For example, you can bring your children on board to get their first taste of the working world. The first $12,000 they earn is not subject to taxes, so more money goes in their pockets.

The Impact of Tax Reform

At the end of 2017, a major overhaul of the tax code became law. The changes apply to the 2018 tax year, impacting how personal and business taxes are assessed. If you have a real estate management company, some of these updates will impact you.

For example, the new legislation permits you to deduct 20 percent of certain pass-through company income from your total taxable income. However, it is important to be aware that a wage and capital limitation is being phased in. Individual taxpayers with taxable income greater than $157,500 ($315,000 for joint filers) may not be eligible for the deduction. If your income is above this threshold, consult your Certified Tax Coach for detailed information on determining your eligibility for this tax savings.

The world of real estate investing offers substantial opportunity for generating income and creating a portfolio of valuable assets. As with any investment strategy, maximizing profits and minimizing taxes takes a certain amount of finesse. If you don't have all of the answers, don't worry. You won't drown in an ocean of tax regulations. Your Certified Tax Coach is always available to throw you a life preserver.

ABOUT THE AUTHOR

Dawn James, CPA, CTC

Dawn James, CPA, is the founder and owner of Dawn James CPA and Co., P.A. She has over thirty years' experience as a tax and business advisor serving small businesses and families across the United States and abroad. Dawn is a Certified Public Accountant as well as a Certified Tax Coach who represents clients nationwide with the IRS and most state agencies. She is a member of the National Association of Tax Preparers and the Maryland Society of Accounting and Tax Professionals.

Dawn's passion is helping people and businesses keep more of what they earn through strategic tax planning and business development. She ensures that she is always on top of changes to tax laws and regulations by engaging in frequent professional development training and networking with her peers.

Dawn's primary focus is providing personalized professional services to businesses and the people who own them, with a special interest in serving real estate professionals and contractors. She also specializes in tax resolution.

Dawn partners with her clients to develop customized processes and automated solutions by integrating their businesses' needs with their individual work styles. She teaches strategies to her clients to improve their financial health through defining their goals, implementing best practices for operational efficiency, and developing budgets and business plans. This helps them manage their time and maximize their profits, ultimately creating a better work and life balance.

Dawn James, CPA, CTC

Dawn James CPA and Co., P.A.

📞 (410) 769-8866

📍 1301 York Road, Suite 303 Lutherville, Maryland 21093

🌐 www.dawnjamescpa.com

✉ dawn@dawnjamescpa.com

CHAPTER 10

Cost Segregation: Your Lifeboat in a Sea of Property Taxes

JAYA R. DAHAL, CPA, CTC

G etting your tax bill down to the bare minimum means finding and plugging every leak. A truly comprehensive tax savings strategy incorporates all available tactics, including sophisticated tax reduction methods that most taxpayers shy away from. The cost segregation method of calculating depreciation expense is one such tactic.

Correct application of cost segregation is one of the most complicated areas of tax regulation, and many experienced accountants won't even attempt to sort through this topic. Instead, they refer you to a Certified Tax Coach or a specialist in cost segregation to ensure your returns are complete and accurate. Despite the complexity of applying cost segregation, when done appropriately, the benefits largely outweigh the drawbacks. When depreciation is calculated through cost segregation, you can look forward to significant tax savings.

The Life Saving Power of Cost Segregation

Owning commercial real estate comes with a long list of responsibilities, from maintenance and repairs to collecting rental payments. In addition, you are accountable for a number of financial tasks, such as securing appropriate insurance and meeting tax obligations. Fortunately, there are plenty of benefits to offset the responsibilities of real estate investment. One of the most rewarding is the opportunity to save on taxes by employing cost segregation. Before you approach your Certified Tax Coach to discuss cost segregation, spend some time becoming familiar with how this method of calculating depreciation works.

As you know, the value of your assets depreciates over time, and that depreciation is generally a deductible expense for tax purposes. The depreciation expense is determined by measuring the useful life of the asset, then dividing the asset's value by the years of service it is expected to provide. Of course, individuals don't have discretion in determining the expected useful life of a particular asset.

There are very specific depreciation periods spelled out in various sections of the tax code. Non-residential buildings are depreciated over 39 years, while residential buildings are depreciated over 27.5 years. It is common for taxpayers to combine all components of a particular property for the purposes of depreciation. As a result, everything from landscaping to outbuildings is depreciated based on the 39-year or 27.5-year figure.

The underlying philosophy of cost segregation is that all components of a property do not necessarily depreciate at the same rate. Certain features should not be depreciated over the same lengthy time period assigned to commercial and residential buildings. Some improvements fall into other categories, and related depreciation expenses can be deducted over a significantly shorter time span. This condensed depreciation benefits you by increasing your deductions and decreasing your taxable income, resulting in a lower tax bill.

Cost segregation is a tax savings technique that is intended for use with commercial property. For the purposes of this tax reduction tactic, commercial real estate is defined as real estate you own with the intention of generating income. Common examples include hotels, office buildings, warehouses, shopping centers, and manufacturing plants.

Typically, there is far more to commercial properties than a single building. One parcel may include land, multiple structures, and additional improvements that are either purchased for or constructed on the property. These are collectively referred to as real property. Through cost segregation, you separate each element of the real property package into appropriate depreciation categories, for example personal property assets and land improvements. These categories can be depreciated faster than the primary building.

Instead of taking depreciation deductions for the entire property over 39 years, personal property assets and land improvements may be eligible for depreciation over fifteen years or less. When the expenses can be depreciated over a shorter period, you enjoy a larger deduction. Your total taxable income decreases, and so does your tax bill. Through this method, you can recoup the costs of improving your property more quickly, so that you can reinvest in other wealth-building assets.

Despite its effectiveness as a tax reduction strategy, many commercial property owners let this opportunity pass them by. The technique is simply not well understood, and they worry about drawing unwanted attention from the IRS.

Clear instruction for applying cost segregation is not available in the tax code. Instead, procedures for correct application have developed over time through a series of IRS rulings in individual cases. It is critical to engage an expert in this area of tax regulation if you plan to apply cost segregation techniques properly.

Inside the IRS: The Truth About Cost Segregation

Many commercial property owners who are eligible to use cost segregation steer clear of the opportunity, because they are concerned about a negative reaction from the IRS. They have the impression that this technique is tantamount to exploiting a loophole, and they don't want their returns flagged for an audit. However, the perception that the IRS considers cost segregation an "aggressive" stance is not accurate. On multiple occasions, the IRS has decided cases in favor of this method, making it clear that cost segregation is not just the most tax savvy but the most accurate way to measure depreciation.

The misconception is likely a result of the agency's firm stance on methodology. Choosing to apply cost segregation is not an issue, but how you classify assets and apply depreciation must be accurate. The process of assigning assets to depreciation categories is known as a cost segregation study. There are clear, published guidelines on performing such a study according to approved IRS procedure. You can find the IRS Cost Segregation Audit Techniques Guide on the IRS website.

The safest way to ensure that you meet all of the requirements included in the guide is to hire a qualified Cost Segregation Professional. These experts have specialized knowledge of and experience in applying approved cost segregation practices, so you can be confident that your returns will pass an examination by the IRS.

Categorizing Assets with a Cost Segregation Study

A professional cost segregation study is the most effective way to accurately separate personal property from real property. As a general rule, elements that fall under the category of personal property are non-structural components of the buildings and grounds. Indirect construction costs and exterior land improvements may also be included under this heading. Non-structural components are attached to the building, but they are not related to operating or maintaining it.

The process of completing a cost segregation study includes in-depth examination of the structures on the property. Expert Cost Segregation Professionals review engineering and financial records, among other documents, to ensure a thorough understanding of your real property before finalizing their evaluation.

The level of detail may surprise you, particularly when you see the results. It is common for clients to discover that unexpected components of their buildings qualify as personal property. More assets classified in the personal property column is good news for you, as you can depreciate their value over a shorter period. That means higher deductible depreciation and a lower tax bill.

This is just one example of the savings available through cost segregation:

Through your business, you purchase a building for $2 million. According to the appraisal, 15 percent of the property value is from the land. You prefer to avoid cost segregation, so you simply depreciate the building's value, $1.7 million, over the required 39 years.

If you had elected the cost segregation method, you might have learned through a cost segregation study that $225,000 of your purchase price can be classified as land improvements. This is personal property for the purposes of depreciation, which you can deduct over 15 years. Another $200,000 is classified as another type of personal property that can be depreciated over five years.

Your new depreciation schedule is markedly different. Instead of depreciating $1.7 million over 39 years, you are now including just $1.275 million in the 39-year category. Approximately 25 percent or $425,000 qualifies for an accelerated depreciation schedule. In the first five to fifteen years that you own the property, you will enjoy significantly lower taxes. That means more money in your pocket to invest in additional assets.

Cost Segregation Opportunities at a Glance

It can be difficult to determine whether you will benefit from cost segregation until a study is completed. However, there are certain situations that are more likely to offer savings opportunities.

- **Existing Property** – If you purchase an existing property valued at $500,000 or more (excluding land) consider a cost segregation study.
- **New Construction** – If you are building something new and it is valued at $500,000 or more (excluding land), a cost segregation study is a smart choice.
- **Renovations and Expansions** – If you are spending $500,000 or more to upgrade your property, you could realize significant tax savings through cost segregation.

- **Leasehold Improvements** – Your tenants may decide that renovations and improvements are needed to suit the needs of their business. Unless otherwise specified, they are responsible for the expenses associated with customizing the space, and of course, they are entitled to use of the improvements while they occupy the building. However, once they vacate the premises, ownership of the updates in the unit transfers to you. If the renovations are made three or more years after you begin generating rental income from the building, and you are not related to the tenants who made the improvements, you may benefit from significant tax savings through cost segregation.

- **Inherited Property** – Many people who acquire property through an estate assume that since the original owner already went through the depreciation process, the option is no longer available. However, this is a misconception. When you take ownership of real property that is transferred from an estate, you may be able to take depreciation deductions based on the property's current fair market value.

- **Look-Backs from 1986 to Present** – Despite common theory that says otherwise, the IRS is committed to honoring the cost segregation strategy. In fact, if you missed depreciation deductions you should have taken on property placed into service after 1986, you still have an opportunity to correct the oversight. When you discover that you should have used cost segregation, you can claim missed depreciation on a current return without amending your tax returns for the prior years.

You have the option of conducting a cost segregation study at any time during the period that you own a property. However, your tax savings are greater if you start classifying assets as soon as you purchase or build new real estate. Your Cost Segregation Professional may even suggest an evaluation during the pre-construction phase of new property, before the infrastructure is in place, to ensure that you maximize your savings and minimize your taxes.

Eligibility Criteria for Cost Segregation Benefits

Every deduction opportunity comes with eligibility criteria and cost segregation is no exception. Before you engage a Cost Segregation Professional, consider whether you qualify for benefits. These are the five most important points to review before commissioning a cost segregation study:

- **Business Structure** – The entity used to structure your business determines your tax rate and your subsequent tax expense. For example, sole proprietorships and corporations are taxed very differently. This impacts the savings potential of cost segregation. Specifically, some companies do not have the necessary tax basis to support accelerated depreciation deductions. Businesses organized as S-Corporations with limited shareholders often come up against limits on the amount of tax losses they can claim. C-Corporations with net operating losses are also unlikely to be able to take full advantage of accelerated depreciation. In both cases, the expense and effort of a cost segregation study is unlikely to offer a return on investment.

- **Strategic Plan** – Your short-term and long-term plans for the property play a part in determining whether cost segregation is right for you. If you purchased real property as a short-term investment, using cost segregation for depreciation may be unnecessary. While you can certainly use this method to increase your depreciation deductions while you own the property, if you sell shortly thereafter, the tax benefits may be recaptured.

- **Type of Business** – The type of business you operate directly affects your ability to leverage the increased deductions available through cost segregation. This is particularly true if you are governed by passive activity loss (PAL) rules. Work with your Certified Tax Coach to determine whether and how PAL rules impact your tax calculations before moving forward with a cost segregation study.

- **Alternative Minimum Tax** – Taxpayers who are subject to the alternative minimum tax (AMT) may not be eligible for the accelerated depreciation deductions available through cost segregation. If AMT applies to you, consult your tax advisor before investing in a cost segregation study.
- **Building Value** – The final point to consider is the value of your commercial real estate. As your Cost Segregation Professional will tell you, the biggest benefits apply to properties valued at $1 million or more, excluding land. However, if you spend $500,000 or more on buildings, renovations, or building expansions, you may realize some tax savings.

These five points are useful in determining whether to pursue cost segregation to hold back the tide of commercial property taxes. Your Certified Tax Coach will offer the guidance you need to select the option that best fits your situation.

Securing a Skilled Cost Segregation Professional

Staying well within the IRS requirements for cost segregation requires careful focus on process. The best way to ensure you comply with all policies and procedures is to conduct your cost segregation study with the help of a Cost Segregation Professional. These individuals specialize in cost segregation analysis, which makes them uniquely capable of categorizing each element of your property accurately.

These are a few of the qualifications to look for as you consider candidates:

- A deep understanding of construction and engineering is critical for properly evaluating a property in a cost segregation study. Make sure your Cost Segregation Professional has education and experience in both.
- Knowledge of relevant tax regulations and a commitment to staying current with changes is a must. Adjustments to the tax

code occur regularly, and compliance requires up-to-date information.

- The candidate you select should be familiar with relevant case law, which makes up a majority of the available guidance for cost segregation. Assets that appear identical can be classified differently depending on the scenario.

- Cost Segregation Professionals are expected to be experts in the process of classifying assets according to the IRS Audit Techniques Guide. Make sure that the individual you select is familiar with the guide and will apply all relevant methods and principles.

Though your Cost Segregation Professional must, at minimum, specialize in this area of tax regulation, it can be helpful to choose an expert who has other skill sets as well. Experienced professionals may identify additional opportunities for you to minimize your taxes during the cost segregation study process. For example, you may learn that you could benefit from Fixed Asset Studies or Abandonment Studies. As a member of the AICTP, your Certified Tax Coach has access to a list of approved professionals who can help you move forward with your study.

Step-by-Step Guide to Your Cost Segregation Study

The first thing to be aware of when commissioning a cost segregation study is that the project takes time. There are a number of tasks that must be completed before your Cost Segregation Professional can provide an accurate report. These are the steps your Cost Segregation Professional will take during the study process:

- Studies typically begin with a visual inspection of the entire property. Your Cost Segregation Professional will take this opportunity to note anything unusual about the building's construction or the building itself. If atypical elements are observed, plan to discuss them in greater detail. They are likely to become an important component of the final report.

- Your Cost Segregation Professional will pay close attention to features that may be classified as non-structural building components or tangible personal property. Since these are the features that may qualify for accelerated depreciation, the focus will be on their purpose and function.

- A substantial amount of time is spent reviewing documentation related to the property, including as-built reports, blueprints, and appraisals. This data supports the final categorization of a property's various components.

- Most Cost Segregation Professionals photograph each aspect of the property and its components, particularly those that may qualify as non-structural building components or tangible personal property. The visual record offers helpful documentation in case of a challenge to your deductions.

- Once all of these steps are complete, your Cost Segregation Professional will create a report that outlines which items are eligible for depreciation as non-structural building components or tangible personal property. The report will also provide an opinion on whether some of the owner-incurred costs qualify as non-structural building components or tangible personal property.

After collecting all the data and offering an expert opinion regarding categorization of various components of your property, your Cost Segregation Professional will assist with applying tax regulations to non-structural building components or tangible personal property. This ensures you have the guidance you need regarding when and how to take the new deductions. Typically, Cost Segregation Professionals complete the following tasks:

- A schedule that identifies each qualifying element of the property, as well as the direct costs for these items and the allocable fees and overhead.

- An outline of appropriate cost recovery periods based on resources such as the IRC, current regulations, court opinions, and IRS rulings.

- Collaboration with professionals such as your Certified Financial Manager (CFM) and Certified Tax Coach (CTC) to coordinate the reconciliation of the cost segregation results with the accounting ledgers.

- Partnership with your finance team to accurately complete required IRS paperwork, such as IRS Form 3115, Application for Change in Accounting Method and related schedules.

- Completion of a detailed report that provides information on the cost segregation study's findings and subsequent analysis. Reports must follow a certain format to comply with IRS documentation requirements, so this is a critical step.

After all of these activities are complete, you can look forward to the final piece of documentation: a calculation of the tax savings you will enjoy if you follow the recommendations outlined in the cost segregation study.

The Tax Benefits of Cost Segregation

Nuances in your circumstances can impact the level of influence cost segregation has on your taxes. The savings you enjoy by applying cost segregation may be substantially different from those of other owners of similar properties. However, after much analysis, experts have created a table that lists the average savings by property type:

- Apartments 20–35%
- Car Dealerships 25–50%
- Golf Courses 20–40%
- Grocery Stores 20–30%
- Hotels and Motels 20–30%
- Manufacturing and Processing (Heavy) 30–60%
- Manufacturing (Light) 20–40%
- MOB'S/MAB'S 20–40%
- Offices 20–40%

- Research and Development 30–60%
- Restaurants 20–40%
- Retail 20–30%
- Senior and Assisted Living 15–25%
- Strip Malls and Regional Malls 5–30%
- Tenant Improvements 5–50%
- Theaters 20–30%
- Warehouses 5–10%

Your results may vary from these ranges, but the data are helpful in illustrating the benefits of using the cost segregation technique. Depending on a property's value, it is common for tax savings to reach $1 million or more in the first year of cost segregation.

Despite the complexity of the process, this is a tax savings opportunity that is worth the effort. Take the life preserver offered by your Certified Tax Coach and your Cost Segregation Professional to ensure that your profits aren't drowned in a high tide of taxes.

ABOUT THE AUTHOR

Jaya R. Dahal, CPA, CTC

Jay Dahal, CPA, CTC specializes in advanced tax planning strategies for businesses and high net worth individuals. He is the founder of Focus Accounting & CPA Firm, with multiple locations in California.

As a tax strategist for many years, Jay and his tax and engineering team have performed cost segregation studies for office buildings, restaurants, retail centers, warehouses, equipment rental, and many others. His extensive experience with the engineering team and knowledge of current legislation, regulation, revenue, rulings, IRCs, and court cases provides clients with a thorough and supportable analysis. His tax planning methods are well documented engineering and appraisal techniques.

Jay specializes in taxation for restaurant business owners and sole or multiple commercial property owners. His team is aware of the rapidly changing landscape in the real estate field and its impact on your business. His team of professionals are real estate agents who have the knowledge and experience to factor in all the variables to help grow your practice and profits from the day you open your doors to the day you retire.

Jaya R. Dahal, CPA, CTC

Focus Accounting & CPA Firm, Inc

📞 (415) 644-5933

📍 1765 Scott Blvd. Suite 210, Santa Clara, CA 95050

🌐 www.focusyourfinance.com

✉ jaya.r.dahal@focusyourfinance.com

CHAPTER 11

Staying Financially Buoyant Through Your Retirement Years

KIMBERLY C. TARA, CPA, CTC

The financial decisions you make now have a substantial impact on your lifestyle after retirement. It isn't just a matter of how much you set aside, the rate of return on your investments, and whether you pay off your debts. You must also consider how taxes will affect your total income.

By some estimates, income taxes impact the value of your earnings more than any other factor, including inflation. If you wish to maximize your income, tax minimization is an important part of your overall retirement savings strategy. Keeping taxes low ensures you will stay financially buoyant throughout your retirement years.

The Basics of Retirement Planning

There are a variety of investment options specifically designed to make retirement planning easier. Most have tax advantages. For example, some accounts offer the ability to defer taxes on contributions until you take distributions while others permit you to contribute after-tax income, so your earnings grow completely tax-free.

In isolation, none of these programs offer a failsafe method of building wealth and securing your retirement. A carefully planned strategy that includes a combination of investments is far more likely to help you reach your financial goals, ensuring you stay financially afloat for the duration of your lifetime. Your Certified Tax Coach is your retirement planning lifeguard. These highly qualified professionals have the experience and expertise you need to stay safe from the risks of poor retirement planning.

While software and other types of retirement planning professionals focus on how much to save and where to invest, Certified Tax Coaches look at the big picture from a total income perspective. They consider the variations in tax rates for different types of income, and they focus on how assorted tax-advantaged programs can be integrated to ensure you reach your financial goals. In short, they have the life preserver you need to keep from drowning in taxes.

Putting Retirement Planning on the Top of Your Financial To-Do List

Whether and how you prepare for retirement makes a critical difference in your ability to build wealth and live comfortably long-term. These are just a few of the risks you face when you neglect to implement a comprehensive retirement savings strategy:

- **Outliving Savings** – In the United States, people are living longer than ever before. Even with an increase in the standard retirement age, you can look forward to a longer retirement than previous generations. This is great news when it comes to checking off all of the items on your bucket list, but it presents challenges when it comes to retirement planning. Without careful attention to where and how you set money aside, there is a significant risk of outliving your savings.

- **Lower Quality of Life** – Leaving the workforce doesn't mean you must spend your remaining years in a nursing home rocking chair. Advances in medicine and better overall health mean you can count on many active post-retirement years. Make sure you are able to enjoy them traveling, spending time with family, and participating in the leisure activities you love by designing a retirement strategy that offers enough income to meet the needs of your preferred lifestyle.

- **Unexpected Medical Expenses** – Though the hope is that you will enjoy good health throughout your retirement years, there is a possibility that accidental injury, illness, or disease will strike. If your financial planning doesn't account for the expenses associated with health emergencies, you risk putting every cent of your savings into medical bills.

- **Caring for Loved Ones** – Your attention to retirement planning influences the size of your estate. When you choose smart investments that minimize tax liability, you ensure that your beneficiaries aren't faced with a financial burden once you have passed away.

There is no need to take on the challenge of planning your retirement alone. Your Certified Tax Coach and your team of financial advisors are your partners in creating an effective strategy to ensure your income needs are met and your tax bill stays low during your retirement years.

Retirement Plans That Support Your Tax Reduction Strategy

The government has taken particular interest in encouraging people to save for retirement, so there are a variety of tax advantaged programs available. Some investors choose a single type of retirement savings plan to hold the lion's share of their funds, but many find it more effective to combine multiple plans in a coordinated strategy.

Tax advantages fall into one of two categories. The first type of plan offers tax-deferred savings. You don't pay taxes on the funds you contribute in the year that you make your contributions. Instead, you are taxed on the principal and earnings when you eventually take distributions from the account and your tax rate is typically lower.

The second type of plan offers an opportunity for tax-free earnings. You make contributions with after-tax dollars, and your money is left to grow and compound. When you take distributions from the account, no taxes are assessed on your principal or your earnings.

The most common tax-advantaged programs include pensions, 401(k) and 403(b) plans, IRAs, Roth IRAs, Simplified Employee Pensions, and Social Security.

Pensions

Though pensions are a well-known method of securing retirement income, many employers have phased these programs out. This is particularly true in the private sector. If you still have a pension or you work for a company that offers you the opportunity to participate in one, there is no downside.

Pensions are heavily regulated, so your investment is usually safer than it would be in other retirement accounts. Your employer makes contributions on your behalf. Depending on how the plan is structured, you may have an opportunity to set additional funds aside. Generally, pension contributions are made with pre-tax dollars, so you do not pay taxes until you take distributions.

The only caveat to these programs is that they typically come with a vesting requirement. You don't own the contributions made by your employer until you have been with the organization for a specified period of time.

401(k) and 403(b) Plans

Most large organizations in the private sector have transitioned to 401(k) plans to secure their employees' retirements. Instead of making automatic contributions to employees' retirement savings accounts, they rely on employees to contribute pre-tax dollars. While there are limits to the amount an individual can contribute, the maximum annual contribution threshold is much higher than with other tax-deferred savings plans.

Many employers match a percentage of the contributions made by employees up to a certain percentage of salaries. For example, it is common to see matches of 50 cents for every dollar contributed by employees up to a maximum of five percent of employees' salaries. Employees and employers save on taxes in the years contributions are made, and employees are responsible for income taxes when they take distributions from the account after retirement.

The 403(b) plan is quite similar to the 401(k), with two key differences. Participation in a 403(b) is limited to employees of certain tax-exempt organizations, a particular class of employees working for public schools, and ministers who meet a specific set of criteria. These programs are not subject to all of the same administrative requirements as the 401(k), so they are somewhat less expensive and less complicated to implement and administer.

Funds set aside in a 401(k) or 403(b) plan can be invested in a variety of equities and mutual funds. While there is a higher risk with these types of investments, the rewards may be substantially higher than you would see with a pension. The main pitfall to relying on your 401(k) for managing your investments is that some plans charge high administrative fees. This is an important consideration when planning whether and how much to invest.

Withdrawals from a 401(k) are not permitted before the age of 59 ½, unless you have a financial emergency that meets predetermined eligibility requirements. In addition to this obstacle, early withdrawals can only be taken against your own contributions. Your employer's contributions to your account are off-limits until you reach the minimum distribution age. If you do take a distribution before 59 ½ and you don't meet the eligibility guidelines, you will be responsible for standard income taxes on the amount you withdraw, as well as a 10 percent early withdrawal penalty.

There is an alternative to taking an early withdrawal from your 401(k) if you face significant financial hardship. Most plans permit a loan against the account. No taxes are assessed on the borrowed funds, and you make regular payments to return the money to your account as you would with any installment loan. Interest on such loans is competitive, and the interest collected becomes part of your total account balance.

It is important to note that when you save for retirement with pre-tax dollars, regulations are in place to ensure you pay taxes eventually. You must begin taking distributions by the age of 70 ½, or you face substantial penalties.

If you leave your employer, you have options when it comes to managing your 401(k). If your balance is greater than $5,000, most employers permit you to leave your funds where they are. If your balance is between $1,000 and $5,000, your employer may require you to withdraw the funds. However, it must also provide appropriate support and guidance for reinvesting your retirement savings. If your total balance is less than $1,000, your employer may simply issue you a check, and it is up to you to reinvest the funds appropriately.

If you choose to move your 401(k) balance out of your former employer's plan, a popular option is to roll the balance over to your new employer's plan. Alternatively, you can invest in another tax-deferred retirement savings program, such as a Traditional IRA. Reinvesting the funds ensures you won't risk a large tax bill that includes an early withdrawal penalty.

Traditional Individual Retirement Accounts (IRA)

Not all retirement programs are designed to go through your employer. You also have the option to save on your own. The Traditional IRA allows you to set pre-tax dollars aside in a range of investment accounts, and you are not responsible for income taxes until you take distributions.

Your Traditional IRA does not permit the same large annual contributions as the 401(k) and 403(b) programs, so some investors use it in conjunction with employer-sponsored plans. Others rely on Traditional IRAs exclusively because they don't have access to employer-sponsored plans. They may also prefer the Traditional IRA because they want to invest their savings in investment products that are not available through employer-sponsored plans.

Your IRA can hold just about any type of asset, including real estate investments, mutual funds, and individual equities. In fact, the only major exclusions are collectibles, antiques, and coins. As with the 401(k) and 403(b) accounts, distributions are not permitted until you reach the age of 59 ½. If you choose to take an early withdrawal, the same 10 percent penalty applies. You are also held to the same mandatory distribution schedule, and you must begin taking the minimum mandatory distribution by the time you reach age 70 ½ to avoid tax penalties.

Roth Individual Retirement Accounts (IRA)

There are some drawbacks to tax-deferred retirement savings plans. Investors who choose these programs rely on the assumption that their taxable income will be lower when it is time to take distributions, putting them in a lower tax bracket. However, there is always a possibility that your taxable income will go up or tax law will change, making the tax liability higher instead of lower.

The Roth IRA offers an alternative to tax-deferred programs. Instead of using pre-tax dollars to fund the account, investors contribute after-tax dollars. Earnings grow tax-free, and no taxes are due when funds are withdrawn. The risk of increased tax rates is eliminated. These plans are particularly popular with investors who have assets that promise a substantial increase in value over time, because the resulting income is truly tax-free.

As with Traditional IRAs, there are limits to the amount you can contribute to your Roth IRA each year. More importantly, you must fall below a specific income threshold to be eligible for this type of account. Both the contribution limits and the income threshold are reviewed regularly, and they are adjusted as appropriate based on changes in the marketplace.

Roth IRA Conversions

Your retirement planning strategy may evolve over time as your business and personal circumstances change. Though a tax-deferred account was once the most appropriate choice for your situation, new developments may mean that you will benefit more from a plan that offers tax-free earnings. Fortunately, you can transition from one to the other as your needs change using a Roth IRA Conversion.

When possible, the process of converting from a tax-deferred plan to a Roth IRA should take place during years when your income is lower. The amount you convert will be included in your taxable income, and you are responsible for paying the related taxes. Your benefits come later, because your withdrawals from the account will be free from additional tax liability.

Roth IRA Conversions offer an interesting loophole for individuals who are excluded from creating a Roth IRA due to high levels of income. The conversion product does not have an income cap, which earned it the nickname "backdoor" Roth IRA. Those who are otherwise ineligible for a Roth IRA can convert their tax-deferred retirement accounts using this method. This allows them to enjoy tax-free earnings on their investments. Note that income limits still apply to future contributions, so those who create backdoor Roth IRAs may be unable to make additional contributions to their accounts.

Simplified Employee Pension (SEP)

Large organizations consider 401(k) plans to be the gold standard in retirement savings, but these programs are expensive to implement and administer. This makes them impractical for small and medium-sized businesses. Fortunately, there are options specifically designed to encourage sole proprietors and small business owners to set funds aside for their own retirement and that of their employees.

One of the most popular options for small businesses is the Simplified Employee Pension (SEP), which functions like a Traditional IRA. Taxes on contributions are deferred until distributions are taken. However, instead of being owned and managed by individual contributors, it is an employer-sponsored plan. SEP accounts are not subject to the low annual contribution limits of the Traditional IRA. Contribution limits are closer to those of 401(k) plans, allowing deposits of up to 25 percent of annual income.

Social Security

During your working years, you contribute to the national Social Security pool. When you retire, you enjoy the benefits of your contributions. Social Security is a government-backed program that ensures basic income during your retirement years. You will qualify for benefits if you work and contribute for 10 or more years, and you can begin taking payments when you reach the age of 62.

The amount of your monthly check is calculated based on your contributions during the 35 years in which your income was highest. The age at which you begin taking payments and your life expectancy also factor into the equation. By waiting until the age of 67 or 70 to enroll in Social Security, you are assured of larger monthly payments for your retirement years.

Some Social Security benefits are taxable, and that amount is combined with funds from other sources to determine your total taxable income. A careful retirement planning strategy that outlines when and how to take distributions from each of your retirement plans is critical to keeping your overall tax bill low.

Retirement Planning Tips from Your Certified Tax Coach

Every experienced investor knows that diversification is key to maximizing returns and minimizing risk. This same principle applies to saving for retirement. A complete retirement planning strategy doesn't restrict contributions to a single type of savings plan. Instead, funds are invested in a variety of programs that work in harmony to maximize retirement income and minimize tax liability. Here are some of the expert tips offered by Certified Tax Coaches:

- **Leverage the power of tax-deferred retirement programs.** Tax-deferred accounts reduce your taxable income now, and you are likely to be in a lower tax bracket when you eventually take distributions.

- **Maximize your use of retirement programs that offer tax-free earnings.** Choose investments that promise a high rate of return to enjoy substantial tax-free income after retirement.

- **Make the most of employer matches and employer contributions to your retirement accounts.** Adjust your payroll deductions to get the highest possible benefit from your employer. Don't leave any of this "free money" on the table.

- Planning when and how to take distributions is as important as planning contributions. Most tax-deferred accounts require a minimum withdrawal by the age of 70 ½, while those funded with after-tax dollars typically do not. Strategize your distributions based on expected tax rates and total balances rather than program guidelines alone. Carefully consider how various programs work together to create your total income after retirement.

- **Delay taking Social Security payments as long as possible.** This ensures that your monthly check is higher for the duration of your lifetime. Since you must take distributions from your tax-deferred accounts before the age of 70 ½, many retirees choose to utilize those funds first, then initiate Social Security benefits around the age of 70.

- **Time your distributions from tax-deferred accounts.** When possible, take distributions from your tax-deferred accounts in years that you have more deductions to offset your tax liability.

Remember, there is more to retirement planning than a smart investment strategy. Building your wealth requires attention to the types of tax-advantaged programs you participate in, the timing of your contributions and distributions, and how the various plans work together to create your total income. You must consider which programs complement each other and which will increase your tax bill, as well as when and how to pay off any outstanding debts.

Your investment advisor and a traditional financial planner can offer valuable guidance when it comes to saving for retirement, and there is a place for automated software when it comes to examining your financial situation in broad strokes. However, your Certified Tax Coach has the experience needed to tie your entire strategy together. These professionals have the specialized expertise necessary to determine how taxes will affect the strength of your financial plan over time, and they ensure that your tax bill is as low as possible, both now and in the future.

ABOUT THE AUTHOR

Kimberly C. Tara, CPA, CTC

Kimberly Calongne Tara is the President of The Tara CPA Firm, LLC, based in New Orleans, LA. With clients nationwide, The Tara CPA Firm provides tax strategy and compliance work for a variety of firms.

Kimberly and her team prioritize client relationships and reduction of taxes through advanced tax-planning concepts and strategies. The Tara CPA Firm follows its belief that, by focusing on planning for the future and proactively reducing tax burdens, business owners can see both immediate and long-term savings, allowing them to reinvest in their businesses and their families. The firm also provides consulting services and assists in the implementation of tax strategies.

Kimberly graduated from Auburn University and received her Certified Public Accountant (CPA) license. She began her public accounting career in Atlanta, GA, and has a background in audit, forensic accounting, litigation support, and tax. In structuring her own firm to focus on tax strategy, Kimberly saw the benefits of obtaining the designation of Certified Tax Coach (CTC) to better serve her clients' needs. Along with her membership in the AICTP, Kimberly is a member of both the AICPA and LCPA.

Outside of the office, Kimberly enjoys family time with her husband and two children, staying active and serving in multiple philanthropic organizations throughout the Greater New Orleans area.

Kimberly C. Tara, CPA, CTC

The Tara CPA Firm, LLC

📞 (504)513-3170

📍 PO Box 74461, Metairie, LA 70003

🌐 www.taracpafirm.com

✉ info@taracpafirm.com

CHAPTER 12

Docking Your Ship: Exiting Your Company Safely Through Succession Planning

AMIT CHANDEL, CPA, CTS, CTRS, CVA, CFE, LLM (TAX)

For many entrepreneurs, the opening day of their business is one of their most memorable life events. It's a major accomplishment and the realization of long held goals. Launching a company is a time of beginnings, and extraordinary effort goes into ensuring long-term success. During this period, the idea of leaving the organization does not seem like an issue. As a result, some business owners fail to develop an exit strategy during their company's early years, leaving them vulnerable to lower profits and excessive taxes when they sell or retire.

The decisions you make now have an impact on the options available to you when you are ready to move on to other projects. You, your shareholders, and your beneficiaries can lose a significant amount of the wealth you accumulate if you don't have safeguards in place. You don't want your profits floating away. Exit planning is a critical component of your comprehensive tax minimization strategy.

Ideally, you should begin your succession planning as soon as your doors open, but there is still an opportunity to turn things around once your company is well established. No matter where you are in the life cycle of your business, your Certified Tax Coach can help. These experts specialize in succession planning so that you can maximize profits when you are ready to sell, or your beneficiaries can enjoy the fruits of your success without losing a large sum to taxes.

Choosing Your Exit Strategy

People choose to open their own businesses for all sorts of reasons. Some are excited about bringing an innovative idea to life, and others are after a profitable enterprise to support their desired lifestyle. Many are focused on building, reinvesting, and expanding the organization to create long-term value. Even if they don't generate a lot of personal income, they own an asset that continues to appreciate.

Your strategic plan looks different depending on your goals, and businesses focused on building value are managed differently from those intended for creating income. Today's management choices may limit your options when you decide to leave the company, which is why it is critical to consider succession planning as soon as possible. You want to be sure your management methods match your long-term financial goals.

These are the most common ways business owners make their exit, along with the effects of each option on your ability to build wealth through tax minimization.

Staying Buoyant with a Lifestyle Business

It's satisfying when the company you built generates enough income to get your bills paid. The promise of self-sufficiency is often what drives entrepreneurs to take the plunge. Once your business achieves enough success to cover your basic living expenses with cash left over, there is a decision to make. The extra money can be reinvested into the company to encourage growth and expansion, or you can use the additional profit to improve your lifestyle.

Some business owners choose to funnel their success into lifestyle upgrades. They move to nicer homes, check dream destinations off their bucket lists, and pursue hobbies that were previously unaffordable. Their companies are structured in a way that permits them to transfer profits to personal accounts for immediate use, for example a sole proprietorship or an LLC with a single owner. Once shareholders get involved, profits must be divided or reinvested to build value for everyone.

Pulling profits out of the business to fund your lifestyle is a valid option, but it is important to be aware of the trade-offs when you take this route. Focusing your business strategy on short-term profits instead of long-term growth typically means that when you are ready to leave the company, there is little or no equity available to cushion your transition. Selling the business may not be a viable option, so you should plan for the very real possibility that when you leave, your company will close for good.

The opportunities for tax savings are limited for lifestyle businesses, as the most effective tax reduction strategies do not apply. In this situation, work closely with your Certified Tax Coach to identify ways of lowering your tax liability in other areas of your finances.

Building Lifeboats for Your Family

There is a long tradition of passing businesses from generation to generation, and many of today's entrepreneurs still work toward this goal. Creating a successful enterprise that offers financial security to children and grandchildren is a legacy that will never be forgotten. If your long-term exit plan includes transferring ownership to one or more family members, you can look forward to a variety of financial benefits. However, there are several points to consider before committing to this strategy.

First, anyone you choose to take over your business must have both the interest in it and skill to manage it. Pressuring children to follow in your footsteps when their passions lie elsewhere often dooms the organization to failure. On the other hand, family members who are thrilled to have the opportunity may lack the knowledge and abilities needed to maintain your success. Handing responsibility for a valuable asset to someone ill-equipped to manage it leads to bleak outcomes for everyone involved. In either case, it is more advantageous to choose an alternative exit strategy, then use available resources to support these individuals toward a career for which they are better suited.

Second, once you have identified a family member or members who have the interest in and skill to take over your business, think carefully about the impact that transferring ownership will have on family relationships. For example, choosing one child over another when both want the business may cause irreparable harm to both. Make sure that there aren't any negative consequences to family unity before you move forward with your plans.

Third, it is crucial to look at the big picture before settling on your exit strategy. This refers to all of the nonfamily members who have a legitimate stake in the organization. For example, business partners might have their own thoughts about how ownership should be transferred, and the expectations of long-term employees who play a critical role in the company should also be considered. Whether or not they technically have a right to participate in your decisions, they can make it much more difficult and expensive for you to give or sell the company to a member of your family if they choose.

Once these issues have been addressed and you have decided to move forward with transferring ownership of your business to a family member, you have three main options to complete the transaction. You can sell or gift the company during your lifetime, or you can retain ownership during your lifetime and pass the business on as part of your estate. A less common but highly effective technique for Limited Liability Companies (LLCs), Limited Partnerships, and S Corporations is the creation of a Family Limited Partnership (FLP). Through the FLP, you can gift shares of the business to members of your family over time. If you plan well in advance, you may be able to keep your gifts under the annual threshold for gift-related taxes.

The tax implications of leaving the organization are very different depending on the option you choose. If you give the business as a gift during your lifetime, you may be responsible for gift taxes. If it is part of your estate, there may be estate taxes assessed to your beneficiaries. In both situations, you might be able to avoid capital gains taxes if you sell the business.

As you weigh the advantages and disadvantages of each method, bring your Certified Tax Coach on board. These professionals will ensure that you have a clear understanding of what you and your beneficiaries can expect from each course of action. Better still, you can get advice on relevant tax minimization strategies that will help keep tax bills low.

Making a Clean Break

After carefully reviewing all of your options, you might determine that passing your business on to a family member isn't a viable exit strategy. Sometimes, there simply isn't anyone with the right combination of interest and skill, and other times, you might find it is better to make a clean break. In either case, selling your company could be the best possible succession plan. This gives you a chance to liquidate the value you created through years of hard work, so that you can reinvest in another opportunity or use the funds to support yourself through retirement.

In some cases, entrepreneurs know from the beginning that their goal is to sell their startup for a profit. They make an entire career out of creating and building successful businesses, then selling them to make space for their next idea.

The types of buyers interested in purchasing a profitable business include companies who wish to expand their footprint or product line and individuals who want the benefits of business ownership without the risks of a startup. There is even a market for companies that are struggling financially. Some investors look for bargain-priced businesses that they can restructure and make profitable again. By transferring ownership through a sale, you free yourself entirely from the obligations of owning and managing your company.

How the sale is completed depends on the needs of your buyer and your long-term financial strategy. Some choose a simple transaction in which funds change hands, papers are signed, and the buyers and sellers part ways. This is quite common when the buyer is an individual rather than an organization.

If your buyer is another company interested in acquiring your business assets, the transaction could be more complex. These types of buyers have their eye on you because adding your market or your products to their existing business will complement current offerings. When they buy an existing business instead of building out markets organically, the expectation is that the newly acquired company will start bringing in profits right away.

Selling to another business may be more complicated than selling to an individual, because your buyer has established its own policies, procedures, and processes. Your employees must become accustomed to new ways of doing things and your current clients may experience changes in customer service, delivery methods, and even the products themselves. It can be startling to discover that after the transaction closes, the business you built is almost entirely transformed.

Determining whether you will sell to an individual or another business depends on who expresses interest in purchasing your company and how much they are willing to pay. Before weighing other factors, ensure you have full understanding of the financial ramifications of each possibility. From there, you can decide whether differences in offer price outweigh other considerations, like the buyers' plans for your employees, clients, and products.

It isn't unusual to have competing priorities. Of course, you want to maximize your profits when you sell your company, but many business owners are also concerned with protecting staff members. This is especially important when you have long-term employees who have made critical contributions to your success.

You may also want to prioritize offers from individuals who have a particular passion for the work you do, along with the skill to maintain and build on your success. Many business owners want to be sure that their years of hard work are preserved in a lasting legacy. From a practical perspective, buyers with a passion for your industry may be your best option financially, because they are likely to pay a bit more for your company.

Once you have narrowed down your options, pay careful attention to how potential buyers plan to finance their purchase. It is common to transfer ownership through a seller financed plan, and your buyers may expect you to offer this sort of opportunity. Seller financing keeps you involved in the company for quite some time, which may not fit in with your future plans.

Finally, you may wish to rethink working with a buyer who expects you to make drastic changes before the deal closes. Correcting globally recognized weaknesses is certainly a good idea, but customized changes based on a single buyer's preferences can be unnecessarily disruptive. Worse still, if the sale doesn't go through, these sorts of changes may limit your ability to attract alternative buyers.

Splitting Profits with Shareholders

The number of publicly traded companies is going down. In 2017, there were less than 4,000, and most are massive organizations like Facebook, Bank of America, and Apple. Private companies make up the vast majority of all U.S. businesses, and most have five employees or less. To give some perspective, in 2010, there were 27.9 million small businesses in the U.S. Only 18,500 companies reported having 500 employees or more.

Some business owners have hopes of creating an exit plan that includes transitioning the company from privately held to publicly traded. Instead of selling the organization to a single individual or business, they want the opportunity to bring hundreds of investors in. While some firms do successfully transform from private to public, this isn't a practical exit strategy for most business owners.

Few companies possess the very specific criteria needed to be successful in the fast-paced world of publicly traded equities. Every element of financial statements is scrutinized by analysts, and the only organizations that can attract interest on Wall Street are those with proven financial success and solid potential for higher than average future profits.

If you decide that your business has all of the characteristics necessary for a Wall Street debut, engage the services of experienced advisors early in the process. They have the expertise necessary to guide you through your initial public offering (IPO). They are especially helpful with interpreting analysts' recommendations, giving you the opportunity to make any changes necessary to keep your stock prices up. Their advice can make the difference between soaring and sinking in the public marketplace. Keep in mind that these advisors work in exchange for a share of your equity, which can reduce the cash that you pocket at the end of the process.

If you are considering this strategy, be sure to calculate the expenses associated with an IPO. Taking your company public is a costly endeavor, and underwriting fees alone will reduce your profits. Your financial advisors can advise on this angle, and your Certified Tax Coach can assist with understanding your potential tax liability.

Salvaging the Wreckage

Many people who dream of owning their own business never actually start a company. There are risks involved in launching a startup, and only truly courageous entrepreneurs take the plunge. Some enjoy lots of success, but unfortunately, a percentage fail each year. If this happens to you, your exit strategy options can be limited. Selling the business for a profit is unlikely, and it usually doesn't make sense to gift the company to friends or family members. In this situation, it may be most practical to permanently close your doors.

It is also possible to liquidate a company that is bringing in profits, but there are significant financial drawbacks to this exit strategy. You can recover most of the money you invested in property and equipment, but you won't get a cent for the work you put into creating a successful enterprise. Closing your doors and selling your assets should be a last resort.

If you choose to leave the business and liquidate your salable assets, the funds generated are automatically earmarked for paying your creditors. Anything remaining once all debts are satisfied is distributed among the company's owners. While this isn't an optimal outcome, there are some positive aspects of liquidating your business. First, the contacts you made and the experience you gained from this venture will be valuable when you start your next project. Second, you are likely to realize significant tax benefits when your company loses money. Your Certified Tax Coach can tell you more about making the most of this exit strategy.

Sharing Success with Your Employees

The success of your business is, in large part, due to your creativity and hard work. Growing a profitable company requires innovation and exceptional management. However, you didn't get where you are alone. Your employees' contributions brought your vision to life, and it is likely that some have spent years working hard to ensure the organization's success.

Employee Stock Ownership Plans (ESOP) are underutilized, but they offer an appealing alternative to more common exit strategies. With an ESOP, your employees eventually become the owners of the company. The primary financial benefit is significant tax savings for both you and your participating staff members. In addition, employees have an opportunity to enjoy the benefits of owning shares of the company they helped to grow. When you leave, you avoid the complications of selling or gifting your business, and the company seamlessly transitions to members of your workforce. Here are the basics of an ESOP:

- Contributions that your company makes to the ESOP are usually tax-deductible.

- If you borrow to get your ESOP started, a portion of your loan payments may be tax-deductible.

- Companies set up as S-Corporations pass their profits to owners for tax purposes. The ESOP is considered an owner/shareholder with tax-exempt status, so the other owners are not responsible for taxes on profits assigned to the ESOP's shares.

- Some ESOPs allow employees to contribute their own funds. In these programs, employee contributions are not taxable until account holders take distributions from the plan.

- Distributions to employees can be rolled into tax-advantaged retirement accounts or investment accounts.

The earlier you start your succession planning, the more flexibility you will have with the logistics of your ESOP. Some business owners give or sell shares to employees over many years as part of a comprehensive compensation and benefits strategy, while others create the program just before their departure from the organization. In either case, the program can be open to all employees or it can be limited to a certain group for the purpose of succession planning.

One of the most common ESOP strategies limits shareholders to partners in the business, making it possible to quickly and easily buy out any owners who choose to move on. Departing owners sell their shares to the ESOP, which reduces the stress and pressure of finding an appropriate buyer for the business.

There is some paperwork involved in creating an ESOP, as you are essentially starting a trust. The trust then acquires and holds shares of stock for the employees who participate. Your financial institution may be willing to offer financing to fund the purchase of these shares, and contributions of stock to an ESOP can typically be deducted on your tax returns.

The specifics of transferring shares to employees should be formally documented before being distributed to participants. Usually, the business sets a formula for stock purchases or gifts. It is common to set up a vesting schedule, so that employees have an incentive to stay with the company. For example, an employee might receive a gift of 100 shares through a year-end bonus, but the shares vest at a rate of 20 percent per year. If the employee leaves the company after one year, only 20 shares leave with him. The rest are returned to the company. If the employee stays for five years after the gift, he owns 100 percent of the shares in his account.

As with any succession strategy, an ESOP is not appropriate in every situation. For example, companies must be registered as S Corporations or C Corporations to be eligible for an ESOP. Forming an ESOP can be costly, and some business owners are concerned that creating shares for the ESOP dilutes the value of existing shares.

Finally, and perhaps most important, owners interested in using this strategy to sell their interests in a company can only do so if the business is in a financial position to buy the shares. For this reason, you may wish to have a backup exit strategy, just in case the ESOP option is not available when you are ready to leave the organization.

Protecting Your Business with an Insurance Life Jacket

This chapter has been focused on planning for your own departure from your company, but it is critically important to prepare for the departure of others. This is particularly true when it comes to unexpected exits. The loss of a business partner or key employee can damage the organization beyond repair if you haven't protected yourself with appropriate insurance.

Key employee insurance is a little different from standard life insurance. It is a life jacket for your business in case an owner or irreplaceable staff member dies. In the same way that traditional life insurance replaces a portion of your family's income when you pass away, key employee insurance offers your business financial support while you work to recover from the loss of a person who is important to the business.

Small businesses are most likely to suffer a devastating financial setback if the owner, founder, or primary leader passes away unexpectedly. In these cases, the company may dissolve completely without insurance protection. Such insurance is also an important investment when the business is in the midst of being sold. Key person policies on buyers ensure that outstanding payments are covered or allow for sufficient time to locate an alternative option if the buyer dies before the transaction closes.

Making a Smooth Transition Through Succession Planning

Building a business takes a lot of hard work, whether you plan to sell in a few years or stay with the organization for decades. You may use business profits to maintain your current lifestyle, or your profits might be reinvested in the company to create long-term wealth. In either case, starting your succession planning early can be the difference between leaving the business with money in the bank or handing your profits over to tax collectors. Don't leave your exit strategy to chance. Instead, partner with your financial advisors and your Certified Tax Coach to choose the option that creates the least waves for you and your business.

ABOUT THE AUTHOR

Amit Chandel,
CPA, CTS, CTRS, CVA, CE, LLM (Tax)

Mr. Amit Chandel has practiced as a Certified Public Accountant for over 20 years at Canethics, Inc., formerly Focus CPA Group, Inc., where he is a coprincipal. Prior to that, he spent time in various corporate level accounting roles where he found his passion for helping business owners achieve their financial goals and dreams. He helps his business owner clients to grow their businesses and plan for the single, most critically important financial event of their lives—the transition out of their business. Amit also helps his clients navigate the complex tax code and advises them on strategies tailored to their situation. As a Certified Tax Strategist, he is in a position to advise his clients to minimize the tax by using the tax code year after year. He also serves on the Oversight Committee for the American Institute of Certified Tax Planners.

Amit is a graduate of Cal State Long Beach with a Bachelor of Science degree in Accounting, and of Washington School of Law with an LLM in Tax. He is also a Certified Tax Resolution Specialist.

Amit Chandel, CPA, CTS, CTRS, CVA, CE, LLM (Tax)

Canethics, Inc.

📞 (562)281-1040

📍 135 State College Blvd, Suite 351 Brea, CA 92821

🌐 www.canethics.com

✉ amit@canethics.com

or contact Crystal Relinski at crystal@canethics.com

Escaping the Estate Tax Tsunami

RANDY JENKINS, EA, CFS, CSA, CTC

N eglecting to create a comprehensive estate plan may have a devastating impact on your loved ones. In just a few moments, a lifetime of building wealth can be washed away in a tsunami of taxes. Instead of transferring your hard-earned savings to your beneficiaries, the IRS will claim a significant portion. The only protection is a broad tax minimization strategy that protects your assets after your death.

The regulations surrounding estate taxes are complicated and ever-changing, so it is critical to consult with a tax specialist along the way. Certified Tax Coaches have the experience needed to identify the most appropriate tax savings strategy for your early years. Then, as laws change and your family grows, you can rely on these experts to guide you through fine-tuning your plan.

An Estate Tax Overview

Although you have faithfully paid taxes on all of your income over the course of your lifetime, your estate is subject to a new class of taxes when you die. In essence, your estate pays taxes on your right to transfer wealth to another person. Estate taxes are distinct from other costs associated with managing your estate, such as probate fees. These taxes are assessed in addition to any other taxes you may owe. For example, if you leave final gifts to your grandchildren, separate generation-skipping taxes may apply.

The total amount due is calculated based on the net value of your estate, which means the value of assets such as businesses and real estate are included. If you fail to create a solid plan for minimizing estate taxes, your loved ones may find themselves in a difficult position. These taxes must be paid in full no later than nine months after your death.

If beneficiaries don't have cash available to cover the bill, they face hard choices. Some of your assets will likely be sold to satisfy the liability, which may include a cherished family home or the small business you promised to your children. Creating a comprehensive estate tax savings plan now ensures that your final gifts don't cause financial challenges.

There is a bright spot in the otherwise gloomy estate tax outlook. Any assets passed on to your spouse are exempt from these taxes, provided your spouse is a United States citizen and your marriage is recognized in the U.S. Alternative arrangements such as civil unions and domestic partnerships do not qualify for this exemption.

Estate Taxes by the Numbers

The first step in developing a comprehensive estate tax reduction strategy is understanding how relevant laws impact you. The estate tax code is complicated, and there are a variety of exemptions and exceptions that may protect your wealth. For example, estates valued under a certain threshold are not subject to taxation at all. However, the threshold changes regularly as lawmakers adjust legislation.

Over the past six years, the threshold has gone up:

- **2013** – $5,250,000
- **2014** – $5,340,000
- **2015** – $5,430,000
- **2016** – $5,450,000
- **2017** – $5,490,000
- **2018** – $11.2 million

Since 2013, estates in excess of the threshold have been consistently taxed at 40 percent. However, before 2013 this rate varied significantly from year to year. It is simply not possible to predict with any certainty what the threshold and the tax rate will be when eventually applied to your estate. For example, the $11.2 million exemption will expire in 2026, at which point it could be renewed, it could return to 2017's $5,490,000, or it could be changed entirely.

Many amateur estate planners overlook the possibility of another significant expense: death or inheritance taxes levied by their state. Even when you are under the federal exemption threshold, you may be subject to state assessments. The best way to protect your beneficiaries from unpleasant tax-related surprises is to leverage the specialized knowledge of your Certified Tax Coach to create a comprehensive estate plan.

Assessing the True Value of Your Estate

The first step in strategic planning is a careful review of your assets. Once you know what you have, consider how the value of your assets will be calculated for estate tax purposes.

When the time comes, an appraiser will determine the fair market value of each asset in your estate. This includes business interests, real estate, insurance, cash, securities, trusts, and annuities. Other items that have intrinsic value are also assessed, including certain types of clothing, fine jewelry, and antique furniture. Be sure to take all of these assets into consideration during the estate planning process, because their combined total is the gross value of your estate.

Some debts and expenses can be deducted from the gross value of your estate. For example, mortgages, select charitable contributions, and fees related to administration of your estate reduce the total value. In addition, under current regulations, any assets that you transfer to your surviving spouse are deducted. The gross value of your estate less these deductions is the amount subject to taxation.

Top Three Estate Tax Reduction Tips

As with any tax minimization strategy, there are a number of tactics you can use to keep your tax bill low. The trick to paying as little as possible is combining techniques that complement each other. There are three highly-effective methods of decreasing estate taxes. Choose one of these to form the foundation of your strategy, then determine whether you qualify for any other, less common estate tax reduction methods.

Transferring Wealth to Your Spouse

Married couples tend to rely heavily on the estate tax exemption for wealth that is transferred to a spouse. Assets in this category are deducted from the gross value of your estate, which means you can virtually eliminate your tax risk. This is a good starting point for estate tax planning, but it isn't a permanent solution. When your spouse passes away, the issue of estate taxes will come up again.

If you choose to transfer your wealth to your spouse when you die, the unused portion of your federal estate tax exemption is passed along as well. When your spouse passes away, the entire estate is reassessed, and the exemption threshold in place at that time will be doubled. For example, in 2018 the exemption is $11.2 million. If a surviving spouse dies this year and neither has made use of any portion of the exemption, a total of $22.4 million is protected from estate taxes.

The ability to transfer unused exemptions from one spouse to the other is referred to as "portability." It was added to the tax code in 2013, and it comes with an important caveat. If the surviving spouse remarries, he or she cannot use transferred exemptions from the deceased spouse.

This particular portion of estate tax regulation was designed to make it easy for married couples to leave their wealth to each other. However, there are a number of issues with relying on this option exclusively. As mentioned, it doesn't offer a permanent solution to the issue of estate taxes, since the problem crops up again when the surviving spouse dies.

Of greater concern is the fact that transferring your entire estate to your surviving spouse gives you no control over assets accumulated throughout your lifetime. Your surviving spouse can do as he or she pleases with the assets while alive and has complete discretion over distribution of assets after death. This can lead to sticky situations when final wishes differ, and there is particular complexity when the couple have children from previous relationships. Fortunately, there are ways you can ensure that your wishes are honored, even though you are relying on the spousal exemption.

One of the solutions to discuss with your Certified Tax Coach or tax professional is dividing your estate into separate trusts. The most common arrangement permits both spouses to access both trusts, but you may decide on a different setup based on your situation. You and your spouse can take advantage of your full exemptions, dramatically reducing your total tax bill. The trusts make it possible to transfer wealth to beneficiaries other than your spouse, while keeping your taxes as low as possible.

Giving Gifts Before Your Death

After putting decades of effort into building your wealth, reducing the value of your assets before your death can be unnerving. However, the idea is worth considering, as it is an effective method of avoiding estate tax expense. Instead of waiting to share your wealth with loved ones, you can gift a portion of your assets during your lifetime.

Reducing the value of your estate saves your beneficiaries the stress of dealing with estate taxes, and it gives you an opportunity to see the impact of your gifts while you are still around. Think of the special moments you will enjoy in the homes you provide for your children. Imagine the pleasure of seeing grandchildren graduate from college, thanks to your assistance with tuition.

If you choose this method of minimizing your estate taxes, consult your Certified Tax Coach before committing to specific gifts. There are separate tax regulations that apply to gift giving, so the timing and amount should be planned carefully. Otherwise, you could discover that you haven't saved on taxes at all. You have simply incurred the expense sooner.

As with estate taxes, there is an exemption for gift taxes. This threshold is also subject to change on a regular basis. From 2014 to 2017, gifts of up to $14,000 per recipient per year were tax-free. The ceiling increased to $15,000 in 2018. Both you and your spouse can make $15,000 gifts to an unlimited number of recipients each year, and you can make gifts to anyone. You are not limited to relatives. For example, a married couple with three children can transfer up to $30,000 per child per year without incurring tax liability. Over multiple years, such gifts can bring the total value of your estate down significantly.

There are some situations that call for gifts greater than $15,000 in a single year. Students in your family might be struggling with the high cost of tuition, or a friend could incur large medical bills due to accident or illness. The gift tax rate has traditionally mirrored the estate tax rate, and the amount over the gift exemption threshold is deducted from your estate tax exemption.

Fortunately, there are opportunities to circumvent these consequences, making it possible to gift larger amounts while still keeping your tax bill low. For example, you can cover medical, dental, and tuition expenses in any amount without exceeding the gift exemption threshold if you pay providers directly. Another option is to gift non-cash assets that will appreciate over time. For example, you can transfer ownership of $15,000 worth of equities to your beneficiary. In 20 years, the total value of the equities might double or triple, but none of it will be included in your estate for tax purposes.

Finally, you may wish to consider charitable contributions. These types of gifts are often exempt from taxes, and the gift limit is much higher than that of gifts to individuals. You can donate up to 50 percent of your adjusted gross income without incurring taxes if your donations go to recognized public charities, certain types of private foundations, or private operating foundations. Through this strategy, you can achieve a significantly lower tax bill.

Creating Trusts to Protect Your Assets

Trusts are useful in estate planning to manage a variety of circumstances. In addition to dividing wealth between spouses as discussed above, they can be used to reduce taxes on final gifts made to other beneficiaries. Trusts are customizable, giving you plenty of flexibility to ensure that funds are used according to your wishes. Two of the most popular options include medical trusts that set money aside for a loved one's ongoing health-related expenses, and spendthrift trusts that limit beneficiaries' ability to waste their inheritance on frivolous purchases.

The primary distinction between trusts is whether they are established as revocable or irrevocable. When you create a revocable trust, you can adjust the fund and any assets it holds if circumstances change. An irrevocable trust is a permanent decision. You are not permitted to reclaim assets held in such a trust, even if you no longer wish to pass assets on to the trust's beneficiary. As you consider your options for reducing estate taxes, pay close attention to the pros and cons of irrevocable plans.

Irrevocable Life Insurance Trust (ILIT)

The death benefits of life insurance policies are a significant asset. For many, this amount makes up the majority of their estate. The simplest way to avoid estate taxes on the proceeds of a life insurance policy is to create an Irrevocable Life Insurance Trust (ILIT). Your attorney handles the logistics of creating the trust. Once it is set up, you assign ownership of your policy to the trust. When death benefits are eventually paid out, they are transferred directly to the trust, skipping your estate and related estate taxes altogether.

There is one drawback to relying on this method of tax minimization. Your beneficiaries only get the tax benefits if your ILIT is created at least three years before your death. By starting your estate planning early, you can avoid the risk of taxation on your ILIT.

The possibilities are endless when it comes to distributing funds held in an ILIT. Life insurance proceeds can be maintained in the account after your death, so you have the flexibility you need to direct when and how your wealth moves from the trust to your beneficiaries. You can customize the disbursement schedule according to life events, beneficiaries' ages, or the achievement of certain milestones.

For example, some trusts are structured to issue regular distributions over a period of time, while others provide for a payout when beneficiaries reach the age of 18, 25, or 30. Some offer opportunities for withdrawal to fund education or the purchase of a primary residence, and it is common to see trusts that don't permit distributions until beneficiaries graduate from a 4-year college or university. This trust is an opportunity to influence when and how the wealth you accumulated over a lifetime is consumed.

Qualified Personal Residence Trust

Estate planning requires you to make decisions about your primary residence. Will the home be sold or will it be gifted to loved ones? If you choose to leave real property to your beneficiaries, you may wish to establish a Qualified Personal Residence Trust (QPRT) for protection against estate taxes.

Once the QPRT is established, ownership of your home is transferred to the QPRT for a predetermined period. Common timeframes are ten to fifteen years. You continue to live in your home during this phase, then the property is automatically passed to your selected beneficiaries. It never becomes part of your estate, so your beneficiaries avoid estate taxes on this asset.

Of course, as with any tax minimization strategy, there are drawbacks. For example, there are still gift taxes to consider. However, since ownership is transferred to the trust and you go on living in the property, the overall taxable value of the gift is likely to be lower than under alternative options.

Finally, in order to realize tax savings through a QPRT, you must outlive the term of the trust. Your Certified Tax Coach will provide guidance on whether this type of trust is right for you, and if so, how to optimize the terms of your QPRT.

Grantor Retained Annuity Trust

Qualified Personal Residence Trusts are specifically designed to protect the home that you live in, but there are similar options for other classes of assets. For example, the Grantor Retained Annuity Trust (GRAT) shields income-producing assets like stocks, real estate, and businesses from estate taxes. This type of trust is generally used for assets that deliver consistent income.

As with the QPRT, ownership of the asset is transferred to the trust, and you are assessed taxes when you make the transfer. Though the QPRT is the technical owner of the property, all income belongs to you. Most important, the assets in such a trust are no longer considered part of your estate for tax purposes.

If your income-producing assets offer inconsistent or variable returns, a Grantor Retained UniTrust (GRUT) may be more appropriate. The primary difference between the GRAT and the GRUT is that with the GRUT, distributions of income are recalculated annually based on changes to the value of assets held by the trust.

Both the GRAT and the GRUT are designed as irrevocable trusts, and both are created to hold assets for a predetermined timeframe. Once the period is complete, ownership of the assets held in the trust automatically transfers to your beneficiaries. Again, this permits the assets to bypass your estate, which can mean significant tax savings. As with the QPRT, you must outlive the term of the trust to realize the estate tax benefits. Otherwise, it is likely that the assets will be included in your estate after all.

Family Limited Partnership or LLC

Sharing property or a business with members of your family can be extremely satisfying. Family homesteads offer generations an opportunity to know each other, and family businesses allow your children to develop important leadership skills. However, estate taxes pose a significant threat to your beneficiaries when it comes to keeping these assets in the family. If businesses and real estate are included in your estate, it may be necessary to sell them to afford the hefty estate tax bill.

The tax code recognizes the benefits of stable family-owned businesses, so there are solutions specifically designed to protect these types of assets. A Family Limited Partnership (FLP) or a Family LLC (FLLC) ensures that covered assets cannot be lost to creditors, lawsuits, or other unforeseen circumstances.

Begin the process by setting up your FLP or FLLC, then transfer ownership of relevant assets to the new company. In exchange, you have ownership interests in the new organization. You retain control over the business or property as the FLP or FLLC's general partner or manager. If you choose to gift ownership interests to your children, the value of their shares is no longer included in your estate for tax purposes.

As long as you retain your shares, you can still operate the business or manage the property as you see fit. However, this adjusted structure typically requires that you act in a fiduciary capacity for the other owners. You can approve or deny requests from family members to sell or transfer their ownership shares, so the business or real estate will stay in the family if you wish. For tax purposes, the value of ownership shares is quite low since there is no market to sell them, so you can look forward to significant tax savings.

Charitable Remainder Trust

Many people choose to include charitable organizations in their estate planning, so that they can put the wealth they accumulated over a lifetime to work on important causes. Such gifts offer additional opportunities to save on taxes. Instead of distributing the funds as part of your estate after your death, consider a Charitable Remainder Trust (CRT).

CRTs work in a manner that is similar to the other trusts discussed here, however they are used exclusively to benefit non-profit organizations. As with the other types of trusts, once you have created your CRT, the assets you designate are transferred into it. You can realize greater tax savings if you select assets that will appreciate significantly over time.

Through the CRT, you continue to receive income from the assets throughout your lifetime, and you are not responsible for capital gains taxes when the property is sold. This works because the CRT is governed by a unique set of tax regulations. Specifically, assets in a CRT are sold at market value, but the trust is not subject to capital gains taxes.

Proceeds from the sale can be reinvested into income-generating assets, and you enjoy the benefit of that income. Better still, you are entitled to a tax deduction when the asset is transferred to your CRT. Once the transfer is complete, the assets in the CRT are no longer considered part of your estate for tax purposes. At the time of your death, ownership of the assets housed in your CRT transfers to the charitable organization you selected as a beneficiary.

Stop Procrastinating

Over 50% of Americans pass away with no estate plan in place. This condition is called "Intestate", and most states have a state ordered process that is applied whenever an individual should die with no estate plan. In many cases, the state intestacy rules that would be applied are not what the individual themselves would have chosen. This can cause additional stress and hassle for the loved ones left behind. As part of good stewardship, it is very important to not continue putting this important process off. Creating your estate planning documents such as a will, a trust, a power of attorney, naming trustees, naming executors, naming guardians, special bequests, can all be greatly enhanced by working with a Certified Tax Coach and a competent estate planning attorney to guide you through this important process.

Estate planning is critical for your wealth to survive the tidal wave of taxes and fees that come with leaving assets to your beneficiaries. Fortunately, your Certified Tax Coach is ready to throw you a lifeline. There are a variety of tactics you can use to reduce the value of your estate, so more of your money goes to your loved ones and not the IRS.

Make sure that a comprehensive estate tax minimization strategy is in place long before it is time to pass your assets on. Review your plan regularly to keep it current with changes in your finances and changes in your family. With enough forethought, you can ensure that your gifts will be enjoyed by generations to come.

ABOUT THE AUTHOR

Randy Jenkins, EA, CFS, CSA, CTC

Randy Jenkins is the founder of RLJ Financial Services, Inc., whose mission is to provide outstanding service to clients based on their dedication to their three underlying principles of professionalism, responsiveness, and quality.

The experience and enthusiasm of the RLJ staff provide each client with dedicated personal and professional service, while their high standards and specialized staff distinguish the outstanding performance of their firm. It is Randy and the firm's goal that every client is well served by the expertise of the entire company.

RLJ Financial Services, Inc. focuses on clients' needs by designing a plan that will help lower their taxes and providing sound financial advice that clients can trust and rely on. RLJ offers complete financial and tax services to individuals and small businesses, specifically tax reduction, investment services, payroll, estate planning, business services, and QuickBooks. The firm specializes in agriculture, medical, and small business tax and financial solutions.

Due to their outstanding service, RLJ Financial Services, Inc. has earned respect from individual clients, local businesses, and the surrounding community. The firm's loyal clients are the result of their deep commitment to excellence, and much of their growth is the result of referrals from satisfied long-term clients. This is a result of a distinct capability and commitment to respond quickly to the needs of their clients.

Randy and RLJ Financial Services, Inc. ensures that all team members are fully able to give their clients the tools they need to make informed financial decisions.

Randy Jenkins, EA, CFS, CSA, CTC

RLJ Financial Services, Inc.

📞 (209) 538-7758

📍 PO Box 1050 Ceres, CA 95307

🌐 www.rljfinancial.com

✉ randy@rljfinancial.com

CHAPTER 14

Cannabis Accounting: How to Avoid Capsizing in Treacherous Tax Waters

SANDY SUCHOFF, CPA, CTC

Decriminalization and outright legalization of marijuana has reached a tipping point. More than half of US states have legalized the sale of cannabis for medical use, recreational use, or both. The number of states that permit medical marijuana has grown to 30 and continues to grow each year. Recreational use of marijuana is currently legal in nine states and in Washington, D.C. Sales are exceeding even the most optimistic projections, and tax dollars are pouring into state treasuries.

While all of this is very good news for entrepreneurs in this profitable industry, there is a significant problem. At the federal level, marijuana is still illegal. The clash between federal and state regulations creates a variety of issues. One of the most pressing is how to manage the reporting and payment of federal income taxes. Businesses in the cannabis industry that fail to get their taxes paid accurately and on time face repercussions that can capsize the entire company.

Special tax rules apply to businesses the federal government considers illegal, and the result is that many common business deductions don't apply. It is easy to end up on the wrong side of the tax law, increasing the chances of unwanted attention from the IRS and national law enforcement agencies.

If you own and operate a business that "traffics" cannabis – defined by the federal government as cultivating, manufacturing, distributing or dispensing of a controlled substance – it is critical to have the most up-to-date tax information before filing. This is one situation in which staying safe means relying on others. Trust your Certified Tax Coach, a knowledgeable cannabis CPA, to keep you afloat through the dangerous waters of cannabis accounting.

A Quick History of Cannabis in the United States

Today, the United States categorizes marijuana as one of the most dangerous and addictive illegal drugs available, but that hasn't always been true. From 1600-1900, plants in the cannabis family played a significant role in the economy. Hemp was particularly important in the manufacture of sails, rope, and clothing. So important, in fact, that in 1619, the Virginia Assembly passed a law requiring all farmers to grow it. Maryland, Pennsylvania, and Virginia even permitted residents to use hemp as legal tender.

It wasn't until the 19th century that ingestion of marijuana became popular. It was primarily used in a variety of medicinal products, but some people started smoking hashish. Marijuana was denounced in the United States after the Mexican Revolution of 1910. Mexican citizens came to the U.S. in great numbers, and they brought the tradition of recreational marijuana with them. Americans were uncomfortable with the influx of Mexicans, and tempers flared as the economy collapsed into the Great Depression. In fact, the name "marijuana" came to fruition from two common Mexican names: Mary and Juan. Researchers set out to prove a link between deviant behavior and marijuana, offering studies that blamed the plant for an array of violent and criminal acts. It is worth noting that these studies carefully linked the use of marijuana and criminal behavior to underclass and "racially inferior" people and communities. It didn't take long for legislative action, and marijuana was outlawed in 29 states by 1931.

Hemp farming regained federal support during World War II, but this did nothing for marijuana. In the 1950s, a series of strict minimum sentencing laws were passed in an effort to reduce recreational use of the drug. Most of these minimum sentencing requirements were repealed in the 1970s, but new, stricter minimum sentencing guidelines were passed in 1984 and 1986.

One of the biggest blows to legalization of marijuana was its placement on Schedule I of The Controlled Substances Act. This legislation was passed in 1970, placing all substances regulated by the federal government onto one of five schedules according to perceived risks versus benefits. Schedule I is reserved for the most dangerous substances. This includes drugs with no medical use, significant safety concerns, and a high potential for abuse. Other Schedule I substances include heroin, cocaine, and LSD.

It wasn't until 1996 that individual states considered taking a stand. That year, voters in California passed Proposition 215, allowing use of marijuana to treat specific medical conditions. Other states followed suit in subsequent years. At first, the pace of change was quite slow, but since the first states passed legislation, the rate of new legislation has increased. In 2012, Colorado and Washington formally legalized the recreational use of marijuana, starting a new trend that is picking up steam.

For the moment, the implications of a change in national policy are unclear, making it even more critical to ensure tax returns are complete and error-free.

The Marijuana Industry in Numbers

Sales of medicinal marijuana have been brisk, but they do not compare to revenues generated by sales of recreational marijuana. States that have legalized recreational use are enjoying a massive influx of cash. These tax dollars are being put to good use, improving education and funding improvements to infrastructure.

These figures show the total sales of recreational marijuana in states where it has been legalized, offering you a glimpse into the financial impact of cannabis:

- **Alaska** $39.5 million
- **California** $2.75 billion
- **Colorado** $1.56 billion
- **District of Columbia** $17.7 million
- **Maine** $83.4 million
- **Massachusetts** $106 million
- **Nevada** $102.7 million
- **Oregon** $777.6 million
- **Washington** $1 billion

In 2017, the industry employed 121,000 people. Based on current trends, there may be as many as 292,000 cannabis-related jobs by 2021. Total U.S. sales of marijuana, both medical and recreational, came to nearly $9 billion in 2017. Sales are expected to reach $11 billion nationwide in 2018, and as much as $21 billion in 2021. States collected more than $1 billion in taxes in 2016, and that figure rose to $1.4 billion in 2017.

There is extraordinary potential for profit in the cannabis industry, but it does come with risk. The best way to stay under the federal radar is to ensure your taxes are complete and accurate.

The Basics of Federal Tax Law for Illegal Businesses

Companies involved in the production or sale of controlled substances may not be considered legal by the federal government, but that doesn't negate the obligation to pay federal taxes. Before 1982, illegal businesses were able to deduct expenses from their taxable income, just as any other business would. The 1974 case, Edmonson v. Commissioner, ensured that deductions for utilities, travel expenses, and rent were permitted under the tax code regardless of industry.

This changed significantly in 1982, when the IRS enacted 26 U.S. Code § 280E – Expenditures in connection with the illegal sale of drugs.

The regulation reads as follows:

No deduction or credit shall be allowed for any amount paid or incurred during the taxable year in carrying on any trade or business if such trade or business (or the activities which comprise such trade or business) consists of trafficking in controlled substances (within the meaning of schedule I and II of the Controlled Substances Act) which is prohibited by Federal law or the law of any State in which such trade or business is conducted.

This reversed the Edmonson decision, revoking the option for illegal businesses to deduct expenses from taxable income. Because marijuana is listed on Schedule I of the Controlled Substances Act, all businesses in this industry are impacted by Section 280E. However, as a cannabis business, there are still steps you can take to keep your taxes as low as possible within the law.

Best Practices in Cannabis Accounting

Careful accounting of each transaction is particularly important when you operate a cannabis related business. Though you are not eligible for the same deductions and credits as other companies, there are still opportunities to save. More important, there are dangerous pitfalls you must avoid to reduce the risk of an audit.

Examining the Core Functions of Your Business

Some cannabis businesses face an interesting tax conundrum, medical marijuana dispensaries in particular. Providing cannabis products to patients is part of the mission of a cannabis business, but many business activities can be related to other types of therapy and support.

One precedent-setting example of this issue occurred in California just after the state legalized medical marijuana in 1996. An organization called Californians Helping to Alleviate Medical Problems (CHAMP) started offering medical marijuana to its patients alongside an extensive menu of additional services. Examples of these services included support groups, nutritious meals, information and education on disease management, hygienic supplies, massage, social events, internet access, and yoga classes. Each patient paid a monthly membership fee to participate.

In 2002, the IRS challenged CHAMP's compliance with Section 280E. CHAMP asserted that the organization's primary business was caregiving services and supplying medical marijuana to patients was a secondary business. To determine CHAMP's compliance with tax law, courts focused their attention on whether CHAMP operated as one business or two. In 2007, the organization prevailed.

The decision reads as follows:

Petitioner was regularly and extensively involved in the provision of caregiving services, and those services are substantially different from petitioner's provision of medical marijuana. By conducting its recurring discussion groups, regularly distributing food and hygiene supplies, advertising and making available the services of personal counselors, coordinating social events and field trips, hosting educational classes, and providing other social services, petitioner's caregiving business stood on its own, separate and apart from petitioner's provision of medical marijuana.

Other businesses have attempted to implement this strategy with less success. One of the more notable was Martin Olive and his dispensary, The Vapor Room Herbal Center. Olive opened his business in 2004, and he elected to provide a variety of complimentary benefits to his customers. In addition to sale of marijuana, The Vapor Room offered books, art supplies, games, social activities, and yoga classes. In this case, the Ninth Circuit decided against Olive, stating that his decision to provide free services to his patrons did not qualify as an additional line of business.

The takeaway from these two examples is this: a legitimate business is designed to make a profit. Services provided without charge may qualify as good marketing, but they do not constitute a separate line of business for tax purposes. If you offer a variety of services and cannabis makes up just a portion of your total revenue, you may qualify for some federal tax deductions and credits for the activities that are unrelated to cannabis.

Addressing State and Local Tax Expenses

Businesses pay a variety of taxes to their state and local governments. Under other circumstances, these tax expenses can be deducted on your federal income tax returns. However, as a result of Section 280E, this is not true for companies in the cannabis industry. There are three taxes that must be added back when you complete your federal returns:

- **Excise Taxes** – This is the tax you pay on the purchase of cannabis. It may be calculated as a percentage of your sales or based on the dry weight of the product.

- **State Sales Taxes** – Some states may assess higher sales tax rates for cannabis-related products.

- **Local Sales Taxes** – Certain municipalities assess a separate tax for cannabis sold at the local level.

Consult your Certified Tax Coach to ensure your federal returns do not include deductions for state and local taxes.

Managing Cost of Goods Sold

The Tax Court had asserted that with respect to 280E, Cost of Goods Sold is not deemed to be a deduction, but rather it is an adjustment to arriving at Gross Income. Accordingly, this technicality affords cannabis businesses some relief. Cannabis businesses are only allowed to deduct Cost of Goods Sold and nothing else. A Standard accounting practices require the subtraction of cost of goods sold from total income to arrive at the appropriate gross income figure. It is not subtracted from gross income as an expense after the fact.

Companies focused on the cultivation and manufacture of cannabis benefit most from this interpretation of accounting practices. Retail businesses still find themselves quite limited when it comes to options for minimizing taxes.

Understanding the Impact of Inventory

Keeping taxes low requires careful attention to how cost of goods sold is calculated. You may be able to deduct some inventory as cost of goods sold, but you must use an inventory method to ensure compliance with IRS regulations. Specifically, you must have clear, accurate records of your beginning and ending inventory when it comes to production, purchase, and sales. Your inventories include raw materials, supplies acquired for sale, partially finished goods, and finished goods.

Businesses subject to the provisions of Section 280E are encouraged to use an accounting or inventory method that allocates the largest possible amount of inventory to cost of goods sold. This technique ensures maximum impact to your final tax expenses. The full absorption method of inventory costing is one of the best options for this purpose.

The full absorption method of inventory costing is defined under IRC 1.471-11. This regulation requires that you consider direct and indirect production costs when computing inventory-related costs. Examples of direct production costs include labor expenses like wages and payroll taxes, as well as material costs like soil, clones, and fertilizer. Examples of indirect costs include your rent, utilities, insurance, and maintenance expenses.

These production costs are allocated to goods you produced during the tax year, whether the goods were sold or they are still in your inventory. You use the same criteria you already established to define which product is considered part of your inventory.

Using GAAP Accrual Cost Accounting

The Generally Accepted Accounting Principles (GAAP) is a body of work that creates accounting guidelines to ensure the financial reports produced by businesses are accurate and consistent. However, unless your company is publicly traded, you are not required to comply with GAAP.

A majority of privately-held businesses choose a cash accounting method, which records expenses when they are paid. For example, if you pay for December's electricity in January, this expense is assigned to January in your records. Revenues are recorded when you receive the funds from your customers, regardless of when you deliver the product. Despite its popularity, the cash accounting method is not supported by GAAP.

GAAP favors accrual cost accounting, which records transactions when they occur instead of when cash changes hands. For example, if the electricity you use in December is paid for in January, the expense is assigned to your December records. If you permit a customer to buy on credit, the sale is recorded when you deliver the product, regardless of when you receive payment. Investors prefer this method, because they know that financial reports accurately reflect current sales performance and the actual amount of inventory on hand.

Businesses that have any relationship to the cannabis industry can benefit from the use of GAAP Accrual Cost Accounting, because the foundation of this method is to match expenses and revenues. As a result, more of your expenses may fall under cost of goods sold. Examples of such expenses include depreciation, depletion, employee benefits, real estate taxes, production-related insurance costs, production-related Officer salaries, and production-related administrative expenses. Including these in the cost of goods sold can have a dramatic impact on your taxable income and subsequent tax liability. A knowledgeable cannabis accountant and Certified Tax Coach can help you navigate these waters.

Keeping Detailed Records

When it comes to tax matters, keeping thorough, detailed records is important for everyone. However, "illegal" cannabis businesses are held to an even higher standard. This is particularly true when applying the principles of accrual cost accounting. Consider these recommended best practices for record keeping:

- Focus on proper revenue and expense recognition. Keep all related documentation available and organized.
- Track the time you spend on individual operational activities in your dispensary. Similarly, keep careful track of labor related to cultivation and manufacturing.
- Don't wait to record and process all of the data you collect through record keeping and time tracking. Complete your accrual cost accounting real time and keep the workpapers that show your calculations.

- Ensure you can show how you arrived at your results by documenting analysis and appropriation of expenses. Clearly explain through your workpapers and other documentation how your calculations meet the restrictions of Section 280E.

Banking options are scarce for marijuana-related companies, which means many transactions are conducted with cash. This is a red flag for the IRS, and high cash flow businesses are frequent targets for auditing. The quality of your record keeping practices can mean the difference between satisfying auditors or dealing with major financial and legal issues.

Filing Form 8300

Large cash transactions are heavily scrutinized by a variety of federal agencies, because these transactions may be associated with illegal activity. Since so much of a marijuana business is handled with cash, you are always at a higher risk of unwanted attention from authorities. Make sure that you stay well within the law when it comes to reporting the receipt of large amounts of cash.

If your business receives more than $10,000 in one cash payment, you must file Form 8300: Report of Cash Payments Over $10,000 Received in a Trade or Business. This ensures that the IRS and the Financial Crimes Enforcement Network (FinCEN) have all of the details they need to identify and prevent criminal activity.

You are expected to complete the form within 15 days of the date the transaction occurred. Forms can be filed by mail, but you may wish to use the online submission option instead. You can do this through the Bank Secrecy Act (BSA) Electronic Filing (E-Filing) System. Filing online generates an automated receipt of your submission, and it reduces the likelihood of errors and delays in processing.

The Complicated Relationship Between Cannabis Businesses and the IRS

Companies that openly cultivate, manufacture, and sell marijuana are a relatively new phenomenon, and many of the criteria typically used by the IRS to initiate audits are simply not available. Much of the necessary data has not been collected, analyzed, and published, which puts auditors at a disadvantage. Unfortunately, when they are at a disadvantage, so are you.

One of the most important tools the IRS uses to identify potential tax fraud is an algorithm that compares gross income, cost of goods sold, and other figures across a large number of companies in the same industry. This makes it possible to determine which companies are outliers requiring additional review. For the moment, this data is not available for the cannabis industry, so auditors must rely on other factors. In general, the high volume of cash transactions puts all marijuana businesses at risk of an audit.

While you may not be able to avoid an audit altogether, you can reduce the risk of financial and legal penalties. Careful, consistent accounting practices and detailed record keeping are the best methods of staying afloat. If you find yourself at risk of drowning in the complexities of cannabis accounting, don't try to solve the problem on your own. Let your Certified Tax Coach, knowledgeable in cannabis accounting, help with the rescue efforts.

ABOUT THE AUTHOR

Sandy Suchoff, CPA, CTC

Sandy Suchoff CPA is the founder of Lefstein-Suchoff CPA & Associates, LLC, DBA The Canna CPAs, which was formed in 1997. She has been featured on FOX News and MSNBC as a tax advisor and has appeared on podcasts and in newspapers in the same capacity. In addition to being a licensed Certified Public Accountant, Sandy is also a Certified Tax Planner, QuickBooks ProAdvisor, and Certified Tax Resolution Specialist.

In response to a family member's health condition, Sandy researched the endocannabinoid system and learned how phytocannabinoids in the cannabis plant can treat a myriad of health conditions with a high level of efficacy. Sandy combined her love of tax and accounting with her passion for the cannabis plant and began to cater her practice to the cannabis space. She is a renowned speaker, lecturing at various national cannabis expos around the country on cannabis tax and accounting. Sandy has also been featured on Cannabis Radio and Purple Haze Radio, and has been featured in newspapers such as the National Marijuana News regarding IRC 280E tax and accounting issues.

Sandy Suchoff, CPA, CTC

Lefstein-Suchoff CPA & Associates, LLC D/B/A The Canna CPAs

📞 833-CPA-CANA

📍 2372 Morse Avenue, Irvine, CA 92614
1350 Avenue of the Americas, 2nd Flr. NY, NY 10019
15-07 Alden Ter, Fair Lawn, NJ 07410
867 Boylston St., Boston, MA 02116
14631 SW Millikan Way, Beaverton, OR 97003
3030 NW Expressway., Oklahoma City, OK 73112

🌐 www.thecannacpas.com
📧 info@thecannacpas.com

CHAPTER 15

Weird, Wild, and Wonderful Writeoffs to the Rescue

MIKE C. MANOLOFF, CPA, CTC

Accountants and Certified Tax Coaches work around the clock during tax season. Once the filing deadline hits, it's time to relax and reconnect with colleagues, family, and friends. One of the most popular topics of conversation is the year's most unusual tax deductions. This chapter gives you an inside look at some of the wackiest tax deductions we've seen. More important, it offers details on differentiating between unusual and illegal.

If you aren't quite sure whether your expenses are deductible, your Certified Tax Coach can help. These experts have the experience necessary to minimize your tax liability without crossing the line into uncharted and illegal waters.

Wacky Tax Deductions That Didn't Meet IRS Standards

There is nothing wrong with a little creativity, but the IRS does set firm limits. These are some unusual tax deductions that were met with a resounding no.

Medical Expenses

One taxpayer suffered from allergies, and she decided to have her carpets removed to reduce allergens in her home. The IRS disagreed that this qualified as a deductible medical expense.

An individual with chronic asthma couldn't breathe comfortably without an air-conditioner. When the one in his home broke, he stayed overnight at a hotel. He tried to deduct the hotel charges as a medical expense, but he was unsuccessful at convincing the IRS that the deduction was legitimate.

Having dry skin may be a legitimate health condition, but one taxpayer learned the hard way that designer bath oil is not a deductible medical expense.

Whether your tattoo is completed by a licensed technician or you have a friend do the work in your home, it does not qualify as a medical expense.

There is plenty of research to support the effectiveness of alternative medical therapies, but that doesn't mean all of them can be deducted from your taxable income. One taxpayer attempted to write off the cost of plant leaf massages and prayer. She was not successful.

Business Expenses

One businessman bought his wife a mink coat, so that she could look her best at company-sponsored functions. When he tried to deduct this as a business expense, the IRS decisively disagreed.

When traveling on business, a taxpayer had to board her dog with a local vet. Though she felt strongly that this should qualify as a deductible business expense, it was not permitted by the IRS.

Burning down a failing business to collect insurance isn't just an urban myth. It happens frequently, though it is impossible to pinpoint exactly how often. After all, most people that take such drastic measures don't confess. However, one interesting store owner wasn't shy about his crime. He correctly reported the insurance payout as income on his tax returns. Then, he attempted to deduct the cash he paid to the arsonist who set the building ablaze. When auditors asked about the "consulting fee" deduction, this business owner admitted everything.

Getting to work on time is important for your career. Even so, the IRS doesn't consider your speeding tickets and parking tickets to be a deductible business expense.

Travel and entertainment expenses are a constant source of friction between the IRS and enterprising businesspeople. Some taxpayers have attempted to deduct expenses associated with a child's wedding under this heading, because the guest list includes business associates. So far, these deductions have been unequivocally denied.

Charitable Donations

Deductions for gifts to charitable organizations are common. However, some taxpayers have an uncommon perspective on the definition of charitable organization. One gambling aficionado attempted to write off his gambling losses as a contribution to the Minnesota State Lottery. Another tried listing gambling losses as a deductible contribution to the casino itself. Neither passed the strict IRS criteria for charitable donation deductions.

There are a variety of quotes and adages about lending money to friends and family. Most of them suggest that it isn't a good idea. If you choose to make one of these loans and you are never repaid, don't expect sympathy from the IRS. Losses related to loans you made to family and friends can't be counted as charitable contributions for tax purposes. They also don't meet the criteria for a personal or business loss.

Personal Expenses

Each year, a shocking number of taxpayers attempt to claim unqualified dependents. For example, one woman listed her tenant as a dependent nephew on her returns. Because this sort of fraud is so common, the IRS pays close attention to anything questionable. This woman was audited, and she had to pay $5,000 in back taxes and a $2,000 fine.

One parent was so enthusiastic about his business-related meal expense deductions that he took it a step too far. He tried to deduct the cost of his child's school lunches, too. Unfortunately, the IRS didn't see things the same way, which led to a hefty tax bill that included fees, penalties, and interest.

Families that incur expenses for childcare while they are at work or school can deduct some of their annual expenditure on their tax returns. However, a family that tried to deduct season passes to an amusement park under the heading of childcare expenses failed to convince the IRS of the legitimacy of this plan.

Along the same lines, a certain passionate dog lover felt strongly that his pet couldn't be left home alone. He paid for a dog walker while he was at work and attempted to claim a childcare deduction. He was quickly reminded that the childcare deduction applies to human children only.

Pets can feel like part of the family, but tax law simply doesn't recognize them as dependents. Nonetheless, a surprising number of people attempt to claim dogs and cats every year. In a related issue, some taxpayers try to claim adoption credits for expenses associated with bringing pets into their homes. Both of these tactics nearly always end badly for taxpayers.

The list of inappropriate pet-related deductions is pretty long, but there is one more worth mentioning for those who might be tempted. Despite their usefulness as intruder alert systems, the cost of owning a dog cannot be deducted as a home security expense.

Though most can agree that the taxpayers in these examples crossed the line between creative and illegal behavior, these attempts were inspired by actual sections of tax code that describe allowable deductions. The following examples of resourcefulness are still unusual, but they meet IRS criteria for acceptable deductions.

Creative Tax Deductions That Were Allowed

Creativity isn't always appreciated when it comes to your taxes, but sometimes thinking outside the box can pay off. These taxpayers carefully documented the reasons for their writeoffs, and ultimately, the IRS was convinced to permit the deductions.

Medical Expenses

A family discovered that the only way to help their child manage severe respiratory issues was a change in climate, so they took action. The child went to a boarding school in Arizona. The family was able to deduct expenses associated with travel, room, and board due to the medical necessity of the move.

Many children struggle with an overbite, but not all turn to orthodontists for treatment. Playing the clarinet has proven beneficial for this condition. Families who choose this option have been successful in deducting the cost of instruments and lessons as a medical expense.

Business Expenses

One scrapyard came up with an innovative way to chase snakes off the premises. Employees put out cat food to attract feral cats. It worked! And so did the business expense deduction for the cost of the cat food.

Professional bodybuilders have a few secrets when it comes to showing off their muscles during competition. One of these is the application of posing oil, which the IRS permits as a business expense.

Charitable Donations

Sometimes supporting a worthy cause takes more than a cash donation, and the IRS recognizes that there are many ways to do good. You can deduct mileage to and from certain volunteer activities, and the costs you incur for childcare while contributing your time may be deductible as well. There are options for writing off some of things you buy for a qualified non-profit organization. For example, if you make cookies for a bake sale fundraiser, the cost of ingredients may be deductible.

There is a fine line between an aggressive tax minimization strategy and illegal tax avoidance. In these examples, taxpayers found perfect balance. If you are drowning in a sea of taxes and you aren't sure how to save yourself, your Certified Tax Coach is ready with a life preserver.

A Little Innovation Goes a Long Way: Creative Tax Strategies that Work

When it comes to deductible expenses, a little innovation can go a long way towards reducing your tax liability. However, it is wise to consult your Certified Tax Coach to be sure you don't cross the line into illegal behavior. No one wants to pay more taxes than necessary, but it is even worse to get a bill for back taxes, fees, penalties, and interest.

These are a few of the areas that taxpayers often miss when it comes to maximizing deductions:

Medical Deductions

Tax regulations are designed to assist with the cost of your medical care. If you have a diagnosed health condition and there are expenses associated with managing and treating it, you may qualify for a deduction.

Some deductible expenses are obvious, like the bills you get for doctor's visits and hospital care. However, the deductibility of other expenses you incur isn't so clear. After all, one taxpayer was denied a deduction for the expense of removing carpets that inflamed her allergies, while another was able to write off the entire cost of a child's boarding school.

These issues are typically decided on a case-by-case basis, and the key is medical necessity. If the IRS questions your return, you will have to prove that the expenses you deducted were directly related to managing a diagnosed medical condition.

One of the most frequently overlooked deductions is cosmetic surgery. Since many cosmetic procedures are elective and not medically necessary, taxpayers often assume that the entire category is excluded. The truth is that there are a variety of circumstances in which your cosmetic surgery could be deductible.

When cosmetic surgery is used to correct a medical problem rather than to improve your appearance, it may be deductible. Correcting disfigurements related to a congenital abnormality usually fall under this heading. For example, children born with a cleft lip or a cleft palate typically need cosmetic surgery to close the cleft. Corrective cosmetic surgery may also be a deductible expense if you are disfigured as a result of an injury or disease. A common example is reconstructive surgery after mastectomy due to breast cancer.

Unfortunately, every procedure is not as clear cut as these examples, and the line between medical necessity and improved appearance can get a bit murky. People who have had significant weight loss know this all too well.

Losing a lot of weight over a relatively short period often leaves patients with excess skin. Under most circumstances, removing it is considered an elective cosmetic procedure, because there is no medical need. However, there are exceptions. If the skin is limiting mobility or becoming infected frequently, the IRS may permit a medical expense deduction for skin removal surgery.

Another gray area in the debate between corrective and cosmetic is the expenses associated with gender reassignment. Each situation is nuanced, and there is no basic rule that covers every set of circumstances. Procedures that are considered corrective for the purpose of treating a diagnosed gender identity condition are often deductible, but there are questions about which procedures are, in fact, corrective. For example, gender reassignment surgery usually qualifies as corrective, but breast augmentation may not.

While cosmetic procedures are some of the most debated among tax professionals, this isn't the only area that gets a lot of attention. Taxpayers have attempted to deduct just about everything you can imagine under the heading of medical expenses. More than one taxpayer has listed costs associated with personal hobbies in the medical deductions category, arguing that they participate in these hobbies to treat their stress.

Dance lessons are an especially popular deduction, as people indicate the lessons treat everything from varicose veins to obesity. In most cases, the IRS doesn't entertain such deductions. They are simply too much of a reach. However, that doesn't mean you should overlook an opportunity. Sometimes, the IRS unexpectedly supports the deduction of an unusual medical expense. For example, one taxpayer's physician recommended low-impact exercise to treat his diagnosed emphysema.

The patient installed a new swimming pool and successfully deducted all related expenses.

The bottom line is that your Certified Tax Coach is the best resource you have when it comes to sorting out which expenses are deductible and which are not. Review even the most obscure costs you have incurred so you can be sure to get your final tax bill as low as possible.

Business Travel Deductions

It's true that the IRS is tough on business travel deductions, and there are some lines that simply must not be crossed. If you get too creative, you will quickly find yourself falling overboard without a life preserver to keep you afloat. However, don't let fear of this outcome prevent you from taking the deductions you are entitled to.

Many travelers attending businesses functions are hesitant to deduct expenses beyond the basics of travel and lodging, but there is no need to limit yourself to such a strict definition of business-related. For example, if the excursions and activities included in your itinerary have a business purpose, they may be deductible.

Often, these outings are intended to achieve dual objectives. They are certainly meant to keep you entertained, but they also offer an opportunity to network with business associates. Examine your itinerary carefully to see how the events are described. If they appear to be deductible, be sure to retain documentation such as brochures and receipts in case the IRS has questions.

The bottom line is that all of your business travel expenses should be carefully scrutinized to determine whether they meet IRS criteria for deduction before you file. In some cases, you may be surprised by your results. One couple was shocked and pleased to discover that the IRS supported their position that their African Safari research trip was directly related to their work as owners of a dairy farm.

If your unreimbursed travel expenses meet IRS guidelines for ordinary and required costs, such as airfare, fuel charges, and parking fees, they should qualify as deductible as long as the total exceeds a specific percentage of your income. There is a lot of flexibility when it comes to what is considered "ordinary," so consult your Certified Tax Coach to ensure you get all of the deductions you deserve.

Blending Medical and Business Expenses

Understanding which medical and business expenses are deductible is a difficult task. When the two are intertwined, there is a whole new layer of complexity. Each year, a percentage of taxpayers submit returns with deductions for medical procedures that they consider necessary for their work.

One of the most common examples is cosmetic surgery that is not for the purpose of correcting a disfigurement. As mentioned, such procedures are generally not deductible. However, some people make the argument that they underwent the cosmetic procedure for business reasons. A frequent explanation is that people who are more attractive have greater success when it comes to getting a job, making sales, or otherwise increasing their income.

Nearly all of these deductions are rejected by the IRS, but there have been a limited number of successes. One of the most famous examples is the story of an exotic dancer who was able to deduct the cost of her breast augmentation surgery. In this very specific case, the foundation of the dancer's performance was the size of her breasts.

The enlargement was far greater than one would find with an average cosmetic enhancement. In fact, the implants were so large that they caused severe disruption to the dancer's personal life and physical comfort. She indicated that she planned to have them removed when she moved on to another line of work. In this situation, the IRS concluded that her augmented breasts were stage props, and she was able to deduct related expenses.

In another example, a wine shop owner argued that surgery to correct his sense of smell was directly associated to his business. He stated that the ability to smell is a necessity when examining the quality of wines. The IRS agreed with his position and approved the deductions.

As with any deduction you take, documentation is key. When your position is that your medical expenses are related to your ability to earn a living, documentation illustrating the connection is critical. When deciding whether a medical expense truly qualifies for a business deduction, the IRS is looking for proof that you would not need the treatment if not for the type of work you do.

Unexpected Allowable Business Expenses

The clothing you wear to work each day is considered a personal expense, even if you have an obligation to wear formal business attire. Under normal circumstances, that means you cannot deduct expenses related to your wardrobe. However, as with many basic principles of the tax code, there are exceptions.

When the business dictates that you wear a specific uniform or costume, it is likely that you can deduct the expense if it isn't otherwise reimbursed. A member of Rod Stewart's band took that logic to the next level. He asserted that the leather pants, hat, and vest he wore onstage were part of his persona for the purpose of earning his income, and he was able to take the deduction. He wasn't entirely successful with his claims that year, though. The IRS did not permit him to deduct the cost of his silk underwear, despite the fact that he made the same argument.

Though pet-related expenses aren't typically deductible, there are deductions you can take when there is a strong connection between the animals and your income. For example, some of the expenses associated with working dogs and cats may be permitted. Certain businesses like junkyards and vehicle impound lots rely on dogs for security. In these cases, the IRS permitted expenses associated with caring for the dogs. Remember that this is not a personal deduction, but a business-related expense.

One business was allowed to deduct the costs of keeping a cat for rodent control after every other option for solving the pest problem failed. In this case, the link was the fact that rodents were consuming and contaminating large quantities of stock. The cat directly contributed to the shop's profitability by preventing these losses.

The more unusual the expense, the more important it is to keep records and documentation showing how the expense is related to income.

To be clear, the income in question has to be included on your returns. One couple kept emus and chickens in addition to their full-time jobs, but they did not declare the income they earned from sales of emu feathers and chicken eggs. When they tried to deduct costs associated with caring for their emus and chickens as business expenses, the IRS rejected their return. After all, it is impossible to have a business expense if there is no evidence that you are earning income from a business in the first place.

The consequences of too many inappropriate deductions can be a full audit of your returns. In some cases, IRS agents go over multiple years' returns because they notice a pattern of unacceptable claims. If it turns out that you took a deduction that doesn't meet IRS criteria, you will lose the deduction. In addition, you are responsible for all of the taxes, penalties, and interest connected with the error. A standard penalty for understatement of income is 20 percent, but in truly egregious cases, the penalties can be as high as 40 percent.

When your goal is to keep your taxes as low as possible, thinking carefully about your deductible expenses is an important step. Some of the costs you incur may not appear to be deductible at first glance, but as you compare the purpose of the expense with your sources of income, there may be a clear relationship. Your willingness to look beyond traditional tax deductions is an important component of your comprehensive tax minimization strategy.

It is easy to take out-of-the-box thinking a step too far, resulting in deductions that don't meet IRS standards. You can count on your Certified Tax Coach to keep you on the legal side of the line with a thorough review of your expenses.

ABOUT THE AUTHOR

Mike C. Manoloff, CPA, CTC

Mike C. Manoloff, PC has the specialized tax planning expertise that you can only get from a Certified Tax Coach. Our unique, advanced training empowers us to find the little-known deductions, hidden loopholes, and proven strategies that bring our clients a boatload of tax savings. We design personalized tax plans to dramatically reduce taxes and preserve income for highly successful business owners, doctors, dentists, professional athletes and high net worth families.

As a trusted tax advisor, we ensure all of our clients avoid attention from the IRS while paying the lowest amount of tax required by state and federal guidelines. Our methods are legal, ethical, and highly effective. Call us today to schedule your free consultation.

Mike C. Manoloff, CPA, CTC

Mike Manoloff CPA

📞 (713)774-7766

📍 6600 Sands Point Dr. Ste. 100 Houston, Texas 77074

🌐 www.taxcoachtx.com

✉ mike@houston-tax-cpa.com

CHAPTER 16

Staying Afloat During Stormy Weather: Surviving an IRS Audit

PETER FREULER, CPA, CTC

From an outsider's perspective, IRS audits are a mystery. There doesn't seem to be a pattern in terms of who is audited and why. This uncertainty makes law-abiding taxpayers nervous. Even if every single deduction is legitimate and you have followed the absolute letter of the law, you could be selected to participate in the arduous process of proving that your tax returns are accurate.

By learning more about the red flags that catch the IRS' attention, you can minimize your risk of an audit. More important, you can ensure you are fully prepared to defend your returns if the IRS ever questions you. Don't allow fear of an audit to prevent you from taking appropriate deductions and using legal tax savings techniques. Your ability to build your wealth depends on keeping taxes low, and that is only possible with a comprehensive, aggressive tax strategy.

Your Certified Tax Coach is particularly helpful when it comes to staying safely away from IRS auditors. Years of experience have given these professionals the data needed to predict audit risk and to fully secure you against allegations of improper tax filings.

A Brief History of Tax Audits

The Boston Tea Party was a pivotal moment in United States history. In 1773, colonists protested British taxes by dumping 342 chests of tea into the Boston Harbor. When the United States was born in 1776, taxes were a major concern, and the original Constitution did not provide for a blanket income tax.

That changed with the Civil War, as the government needed to raise funds for the war effort. President Lincoln and Congress passed the Revenue Act of 1862, establishing a federal income tax. The law also created the original Bureau of Internal Revenue. This tax was repealed ten years later, and a number of attempts were made to reinstate it in the decades that followed.

It wasn't until the 16th Amendment to the Constitution was ratified in 1913 that a permanent federal income tax became law. The Bureau of Internal Revenue was part of that package, and the agency immediately got to work on ensuring that everyone paid their fair share. In 1953, the Bureau was renamed, and it has been known as the Internal Revenue Service ever since.

Until 1997, the IRS randomly selected returns for audit purposes. It also relied on tips from informants, who were often the spouses and business partners of those filing fraudulent returns. Today, the Whistleblower Program is an important component of the IRS strategy to fight tax fraud. Informants may collect a reward of up to 30 percent of recovered taxes if their tip leads to successful resolution of fraud cases.

The audit selection process was completely revamped from 1997–2002. Computer algorithms were designed to identify the returns most likely to include incorrect or fraudulent information. With the advanced technology, the IRS has been better able to direct its efforts to maximize return on investment.

Changing the process for selecting audit targets is still not enough for the IRS to pursue every suspected case of error or fraud. A variety of factors have combined to limit the agency's ability to operate at peak effectiveness. The IRS workforce has declined while workload increased, and in recent decades, the agency's mandate has been to focus on service instead of enforcement. In part, these changes were the result of 1998 Congressional legislation intended to protect taxpayers from perceived abuses at the hands of the IRS.

How Common Are Audits and Who Is at Risk?

In 2018, the IRS processed 147,058,000 returns. This figure represents a substantial increase from the 93,205,000 processed in 2010. Of the total returns processed, only about 1 percent were audited. However, your risk is not 1/100. Certain factors can make your return stand out, which increases the risk of an audit.

Those who report income greater than $200,000 have a slightly higher than average chance of being audited. In 2016, 1.7 percent of such returns received additional attention from the IRS. However, your risk doesn't increase significantly until you report income over $1 million. In 2016, 5.8% of returns reporting income of $1 million or more were audited.

Reporting no income at all is another red flag, and those who claim refundable credits with no income are often asked to produce supporting documentation. The IRS conducts frequent audits of returns claiming the Earned Income Credit due to excessive fraud in this particular area.

Another discrepancy that is likely to trigger an audit is claiming business expenses on a personal return when you work for a company that reimburses expenses. The issue here is that your employer is also claiming these expenses. When your return includes these deductions, it appears that the same expenses are being deducted twice. If your company has a policy around reimbursing expenses and you choose not to follow it, tax regulations consider this a voluntary forfeiture of your reimbursement. You are not permitted to deduct these types of expenses.

The IRS uses a variety of algorithms to automate their analysis of returns. One type of analysis is referred to as Discriminate Income Function (DIF). This compares your return to others in search of anything unusual.

Red flags for businesses include returns that vary significantly from previous years or from others in the industry. Individual returns are compared against others with similar demographics. Examples include income, family size, career type, and neighborhood. If any of your figures are much higher or much lower than those of your peers, you may be selected for an audit.

Individuals who are self-employed may get a second look if their income is lower than expected based on local cost of living. These parameters were designed to identify people who are underreporting income earned through self-employment. If you are audited for this reason, you will be asked to explain how you afford your lifestyle on your reported income, and you may be required to provide a detailed breakdown of your living expenses.

Another common issue is a mismatch between employer documentation and the information on your return. Reporting requirements for employers have increased significantly in recent years to ensure that all taxpayers pay appropriate taxes on their income. If the income claimed on your return does not match corresponding reports from employers, you can expect a letter from the IRS. It is likely that the rest of your return will be closely scrutinized as well. If other information appears questionable, you may be selected for an audit.

There is one type of income that causes frequent issues for taxpayers: income from cancellation of debt. This situation occurs when you received any sort of financial assistance, such as a loan, credit card, or a line of credit, that you did not have to pay back. You may have come to an agreement with the lender to pay less than the total amount owed, or the lender might have given up and canceled the debt to get it off the books. The lender then files a report with the IRS stating you received income from cancellation of debt.

In many cases, these accounts are so old that your copy of the form goes to a long out-of-date address. Though you may not actually owe taxes on the income from the canceled debt, your failure to acknowledge and account for the income results in a documentation mismatch. You can expect the IRS to explore the situation further.

It is important to note that before investing in a full-fledged field audit, the IRS performs a cost-benefit analysis. This determines whether the taxes, interest, and penalties that may be collected outweigh the expense of a complete investigation.

Best Practices for Avoiding an Audit

The most important thing you can do to avoid an audit is to follow the letter of the law. Take all of the deductions and credits you are entitled to, but don't attempt to sneak under the radar with illegitimate claims. An aggressive approach to tax minimization is a good thing. A fraudulent approach is likely to land you in hot water.

Here are a few more best practices for reducing your audit risk:

- **Accurately report all of your income.** Every time you receive a tax form, such as a W2 or a 1099, the IRS gets a copy. If the information on your return doesn't match IRS records, you are likely to be selected for an audit.

- **Keep documentation for every deduction.** If you have mastered the art of minimizing your taxes, your deductions may seem high in proportion to your income. This sort of discrepancy can trigger an audit. However, resist the temptation to skip legal deductions to avoid an audit. Better to claim the deductions you are entitled to and provide supporting documentation as needed than to pay more in hopes of avoiding an audit.

- **Try mobile deduction tracking apps.** Technology is on your side when it comes to documentation. There are a variety of mobile apps that simplify the process of collecting and storing receipts and tracking mileage expenses. Better still, when you are ready to file, all of the information is organized and calculations are complete. You can easily transfer data from the app to your returns.

- **Obtain accurate documentation for charitable contributions.** Documentation mismatches related to charitable contributions are quite common. Many times, the error is on the part of the organization. Any donations over a certain threshold can be automatically denied during an audit if you don't have an acknowledgment letter from the organization listing the date of the donation and the items donated. There must also be a statement verifying that no goods or services were provided in exchange for your donation.

- **Take extra care with certain types of deductions.** Although it hasn't been officially confirmed, most tax specialists believe that some categories of deductions are more likely to trigger an audit than others. Double check that you have appropriate documentation for vehicle, travel, and entertainment expenses, as well as any deductions you take for casualty losses or bad debt.

- **Deductions that don't match your business or lifestyle might raise red flags.** There are a variety of ways to justify deductions for your business expenses. However, you should expect to provide documentation and a legitimate explanation for unusual deductions. If you are an electrician claiming international travel as a business expense, be sure you have accurately documented the business reason for your trip.

- **Be prepared to explain ongoing business losses.** If your business operates at a loss year after year, you can expect the IRS to ask the obvious question: why stay in business if there is no profit? Auditors will be looking for unreported income, so be sure that you stay on the right side of the reporting line.

- **Don't round or estimate your numbers.** Every figure on your tax returns should be accurate, with rounding and estimating limited to cents, not dollars. Perfectly round figures for income and expenses indicate an issue, which invites a closer look from agency officials.

- **Consider electronic filing.** The IRS has published data showing that only 1 percent of electronically filed returns contain errors. The rate of errors on paper returns is often as high as 21 percent. By filing your returns electronically, you are categorized with others who have a low probability of errors. This may prevent your return from attracting unwelcome attention.

- **Respond to IRS letters right away.** If you receive correspondence from the agency notifying you of an error or requesting additional information, follow up immediately. Failure to respond may trigger an audit in situations that could have been resolved quickly and easily. It is common to forget an item on your returns. For example, sale of stock or real estate early in the year can slip your mind by the time you file. The letter you receive is simply a request to rectify the discrepancy. If you explain the error and write a check for the additional amount owed, you probably won't face any penalties.

- **Beware of disreputable tax preparers.** Even the best tax preparers can make honest mistakes, but some have dishonorable motives. Whether they are trying to keep your business by getting you a large refund or they have created a way to profit from your return, you might discover that inaccurate deductions are claimed without your knowledge. You can still be held legally and financially responsible for returns filed in your name, even if they were prepared by someone else. Make sure to choose a reputable tax advisor and carefully examine all of your forms to be sure you understand and agree with the information.

- **Keep your contact information up-to-date.** The first communication you receive from the IRS arrives by mail. If you have relocated and you don't receive the letter, the situation can escalate before you are aware of and have a chance to resolve the issue.

Keep in mind that most audits take place a year or two after your return is filed. Letters you receive today are unlikely to be in reference to the most recent tax year.

What to Expect During an Audit

Many taxpayers have never been through an audit. Their impressions of the process are formed from the experiences of distant acquaintances or references in popular culture. Many of the horror stories date back to the early 1960s, when an extraordinary 5.6 percent of returns were audited and the process was far more arduous.

These rumors and stories are invariably anxiety provoking, which can make avoiding an audit your top priority. This distracts from your true goal: to minimize your taxes. Fortunately, a thorough understanding of the audit process can transform your perspective. Once you know what to expect, you can confidently maximize your use of tax reduction strategies, whether or not they increase your audit risk.

First, it is important to recognize that an audit doesn't necessarily mean that the IRS suspects fraud. While fraud is one reason that audits are performed, the agency may also initiate the process for an error. If it is a simple mistake in calculation, IRS representatives often adjust your returns and notify you of the change. If it appears more complicated, you may be asked to participate in the appropriate adjustment.

There are two types of audits: correspondence audits and field audits. Correspondence audits are much more common, and they are typically triggered when there is a single issue with your return. Sometimes, there is an error that needs your attention. Other times, the agency has questions on one of the figures included in your filing. In a correspondence audit, you receive a letter detailing the question or concern, and you can usually solve the problem with a call and submission of additional documentation.

A field audit is an in-depth review of your entire return. These are the audits that strike fear into the hearts of taxpayers. If your return is selected for a field audit, you are required to meet with the tax examiner or compliance officer in person to discuss any issues that have been identified. Expect to spend a substantial amount of time with the IRS agent. You will go over your entire return, as well as the documentation you filed away to support your deductions.

These meetings may take place at your local IRS office, or you might be asked to meet with the auditor at a tax advisor or an attorney's office. In some situations, the auditor may visit you at your home or business. Rest assured that you don't have to attend such meetings alone. You are permitted to bring your attorney, Certified Tax Coach, or accountant for advice and support. In fact, you can choose to send a representative instead of going yourself, as long as you complete the necessary power of attorney paperwork.

If the information on your return is accurate, and you have the appropriate documentation to support all of your deductions, you have nothing to fear from an audit. However, if it is determined that you committed tax fraud, you may be subject to serious legal and financial consequences.

Four letters to look for include the following:

- **IRS Form CP-2000:** This is more of a pre-audit request for information, correction, or clarification. If you supply the needed information, the matter is closed.

- **IRS Form 566(CG):** This is notification of a correspondence audit. You are typically asked to provide documentation supporting the deductions in question.

- **IRS Audit Notice on Form 3572:** This letter advises that you have been selected for an in-person audit. You will be expected to appear at the local IRS office for a detailed review of your return.

- **IRS Field Audit Notice on Form 3572:** This notification informs you that an auditor plans to visit your business or home to conduct a detailed review of your return.

If you are selected for an audit, there is no need to panic. The vast majority of them are handled through the mail, and your Certified Tax Coach is available to ensure your response is submitted promptly and accurately to avoid further action. If you have documentation to support the information on your returns, it is unlikely that you will be subject to a field audit.

Keep in mind that the IRS is just as prone to error as any other agency, and more important, your previous tax preparers may have made mistakes as well. It is always possible that the audit will work out in your favor. A small but happy group learn of mistakes in previous returns or errors by the IRS, and they actually get a check once the audit process is complete.

State Tax Audits: A Frequently Overlooked Risk

Most taxpayers are deeply concerned about avoiding a federal tax audit. Often, they completely overlook the possibility of an audit by state tax collectors. States are typically held to stricter standards when it comes to budgeting, so their need for revenue is more pressing. That makes tax fraud investigations a high priority.

As with your federal tax returns, you have nothing to fear from an audit of your state returns as long as they are complete and accurate. Keep documentation for any deductions you claim so you can validate your eligibility for the deductions if there are questions. Remember that if you live in one state and work in another, you must file returns in both states.

If you receive notification of an audit, see your Certified Tax Coach and your tax attorney right away. Your Certified Tax Coach can help you collect all of the documentation necessary to ensure you sail smoothly through the audit process. Your tax attorney is there to ensure that you are treated fairly by the auditor and that you don't inadvertently open yourself up to additional risk. Keep in mind that scams related to taxes are increasingly popular. One of the most common techniques is a fraudulent call from individuals impersonating IRS officials. They advise that you must pay overdue taxes immediately to avoid arrest. The callers take your financial information over the phone and proceed to make withdrawals from your account. Remember that the IRS will never request your information over the phone, and initial contact is always by official mail.

Ultimately, your Certified Tax Coach will guide you in taking advantage of the countless tax savings techniques out there to minimize your taxes legally and effectively. If you are audited, it may rock the boat, but your Certified Tax Coach will already have the lifeboat you need.

ABOUT THE AUTHOR

Peter Freuler, CPA, CTC

Peter succeeded his father, Peter Sr., at the helm of the family's public accounting business, Peter Freuler & Associates, in 2005. The practice has operated since 1984 and provides quality, personalized service along with the friendly and responsive assistance you would expect from a family-run business.

Peter is licensed as a Certified Public Accountant in Florida. He holds a bachelor's degree from Columbia University and a master's degree in Accounting from the University of Central Florida.

Peter enjoys being outdoors and traveling. He relishes spending time with his wife, son, and daughter.

Peter Freuler, CPA, CTC

Peter Freuler & Associates CPAs

📞 (407)847-6600

📍 231 N John Young Parkway, Kissimmee, FL 34741

🌐 www.tax-coaching.com

✉ info@pjfcpa.com

CHAPTER 17

Drowning in Taxes? A Certified Tax Coach Can Be Your Lifeguard

YOHAN J. ATLAN, EA, CTC

There are dozens of options for web-based tax services and do-it-yourself tax preparation software. Many of these programs are highly regarded, and millions of people rely on them each year. When combined with the thousands of books, websites, and manuals devoted to the topic, it is tempting to think you don't need an accountant or Certified Tax Coach.

The truth is that self-service tax software only works for people who are content with paying high tax bills. If you are truly committed to minimizing your taxes, you need a comprehensive tax savings plan that includes one-on-one support from an expert.

Investing in a highly-qualified accountant means you are likely to save far more in taxes than you pay in professional accounting fees. Remember, when you are drowning in taxes, sometimes the only way to save yourself is to allow someone else to help you. A Certified Tax Coach is the lifeguard you need to keep your taxes low.

The Risk of Spreading Your Resources Too Thin

There is a reason why major organizations outsource functions like payroll, security, and IT support to third party vendors. These activities require a specialized skill set. Smart company leaders stay focused on their core business activities. They don't risk spreading their resources too thin by taking on all of the tasks related to running the organization.

Unfortunately, most individuals don't adopt this strategy. Instead, they try to do many tasks on their own. They quickly find themselves weighed down by trying to learn and do too many complex projects at once. At best, results are mediocre. Although everything gets done, it is not done particularly well.

Unless your primary area of interest is understanding the tax code, it is nearly impossible to invest the amount of time necessary to become a true expert. Learning the ins and outs of tax regulations well enough to apply them to your maximum advantage is a massive undertaking.

Avoid the risk of mediocre tax savings by leaving your tax planning to the experts. This gives you the flexibility to focus on your strengths.

Maximize Tax Savings with Expert Advisors

Each year brings changes to the tax laws. Sometimes, the adjustments are as simple as raising the contribution limits for retirement accounts. Other times, the tax code gets a complete overhaul. It is common for tax savings opportunities you have taken advantage of for years to suddenly disappear, and new opportunities may pop up at any time.

Keeping up with tax-related legislation and case law is a full-time job. Fortunately, Certified Tax Coaches have a passion for this type of work. These professionals are always on alert for better ways to bring tax bills down.

Hiring a talented accountant gives you two significant advantages over do-it-yourself tax preparation software. First, you can be sure you are using the most effective tax minimization strategy for your unique circumstances. Second, and equally important, your accountant will ensure that you don't claim deductions or employ tax strategies that are prohibited by tax regulations. Though tax minimization is your primary goal, avoiding penalties and fees from an audit with poor results is probably a close second.

Sometimes, you have to engage in creative thinking to connect your expenses with legitimate deductions. Experienced accountants know whether your creativity meets IRS standards or crosses the line into dangerous waters. They know what has worked for past clients, and they have a sense of how tax laws are generally interpreted when the language isn't clear-cut.

Effective accountants are well-versed in case law, and they carefully follow new developments to ensure they have the most up-to-date information when advising on your situation. If they don't know an answer offhand, they know where to find it. They can typically tap into a network of professional contacts for detailed information, and they belong to professional organizations that connect them with an array of resources.

Short-term advice is just the beginning. A skilled accountant understands that reaching your financial goals requires a long-term plan. These professionals can advise on the best way to structure your business, whether cost segregation is appropriate for your situation, and how to manage your expanding business without losing your increased profits to taxes.

No matter how much time you put into learning the ins and outs of tax law yourself, it is simply not possible to recreate the depth and breadth of knowledge that an experienced accountant has. Taken as a whole, the tax code may be the most complex set of laws in the country. It is easy to drown when you try to navigate it alone.

What to Consider When Choosing an Accountant

Whether you are in the highest tax bracket or the lowest, saving money on taxes is key to building your wealth long-term. An experienced accountant can help you reach your financial goals. However, as with any relationship, some matches are more effective than others. You need to ensure that you and your accountant are on the same page when it comes to your business, and that your accountant has the appropriate qualifications needed to ensure a successful partnership.

Average Results vs. Extraordinary Results

Millions of tax returns are filed each year, and there are plenty of accountants who focus on volume. They churn through returns rapidly, sticking with basic deductions and getting average results. That's fine for taxpayers who aren't concerned with keeping their taxes as low as possible, but it's not right for you or your business. Interview potential accountants to determine whether their priorities and underlying tax philosophy match yours.

The following three techniques are the most critical strategies for saving on taxes. Your ideal accountant is willing and able to maximize all three when working with your returns.

Turning High-Tax Income into Low-Tax Income

The wealth you have already accumulated is important in your financial planning, but for tax purposes, your current sources of income can be more important. Tax rates vary greatly depending on where your earnings come from. A skilled accountant can help you save by shifting the source of your earnings from high-tax categories to low-tax categories. In some cases, taxpayers have completely transformed their tax situation by creating a brand new business.

Make sure that the accountant you choose is familiar with minimizing taxes by maximizing low-tax and no-tax sources of income. Then, check to be certain that he or she is comfortable advising in this area. When it comes to minimizing your taxes, you need a partner who is willing to share ideas and opinions. If your accountant simply follows your directions, then you are no better off than if you do the work yourself.

Timing is Everything

Investors always hope to time the market to their best advantage, putting money in when prices are low, so they can earn a profit when prices go up. Your tax minimization strategy relies on the same principle. Good accountants point you in the right direction when it comes to building your portfolio. Great ones offer advice on timing deductions, sales, and distributions to keep your tax bill low.

As you interview accountants, ask about their experience with giving this sort of advice. Do they understand timing strategies and how to apply them in your situation? Their ability to guide you on applying tax regulations when the timing benefits you most can make a dramatic difference in your final tax bill.

In-Depth Knowledge of Tax Law

Staying current with tax regulations is always a challenge. The application of various laws changes constantly as individual cases are decided in court and precedents are set. In addition, there is new legislation that must be reviewed and analyzed every year. Filing 2018 returns promises to be especially tricky, as Congress passed a massive tax overhaul that rolled out this year.

It is a full-time job to stay on top of changes in the tax law, and your ideal accountant is one who makes this a priority. Unless you are an accountant yourself, it simply isn't practical to do this research on your own. Choose an accountant who has an in-depth understanding of current tax code and knows how recent changes will impact individual returns. More importantly, make sure your accountant is comfortable applying these regulations to real-world scenarios to maximize tax savings.

Risk tolerance is a term used when describing the characteristics of individual investors. Skilled investment advisors steer clients towards assets that match their level of comfort with the balance of risk vs. reward. This term can also be applied to taxpayers. Some are willing to push the boundaries of tax law for unusual deductions, even if the risk of an audit increases. Others prefer to play it safe, passing up opportunities to save on taxes in favor of avoiding unwanted attention from auditors.

The success of your relationship with your accountant depends on how well you are matched when it comes to taking risks. Some accountants will support you in taking creative deductions if they believe they can make a valid argument that the deductions are legal. Others prefer to avoid the argument altogether by sticking with tax strategies that have been tested many times before. Choose an accountant whose risk tolerance is similar to yours, so that you can work together to identify opportunities for tax savings.

Combining Basic Skills with Specialized Experience

A lot goes into securing a state accounting license, but that doesn't mean all licensed accounting professionals are equally skilled. It is possible to earn a license and still make substantial errors or give bad advice. Make sure the accountant you choose has basic qualifications, then go a step further to ensure that he or she knows how to apply their knowledge and skill for your benefit.

All accountants must pass a difficult four-part exam before they can practice. Areas covered in the test include auditing and attestation, financial accounting and reporting, business environment and concepts, and regulation. Of course, as with any exam, once the test is over and results are in, it is easy to forget a lot of the details if knowledge isn't applied on a regular basis.

State Boards of Accountancy and national professional organizations require accountants to complete continuing education classes to maintain their licenses. However, accountants that don't typically work in tax minimization for people in your situation are unlikely to learn or retain the information needed to give you appropriate guidance.

When interviewing possible accountants, ask about their experience and expertise in the area of tax law that applies to you. For business owners, does the accountant work on a lot of business returns, or is their primary focus on personal returns? Does the accountant have other clients in your industry? Does he or she work primarily with sole proprietors or corporations?

There are substantial differences in the application of tax laws between industries and business entities. For example, deductions for a real estate agency are quite different from deductions for a home day care. If your candidate doesn't have experience working with others in situations similar to yours, you may miss out on advice that is critical for keeping your tax bill low.

Next, consider your needs when it comes to tax preparation versus tax planning. Some accountants only offer tax preparations services, while others do both. If you have a team of people to advise you on your financial affairs, you may only need an accountant who can prepare your returns. However, if you are relying on your accountant to offer in-depth counseling on tax minimization strategies, be sure you choose a professional with the appropriate skill set.

Note the following differences between tax preparation and tax planning.

Tax Preparation Responsibilities

- Manages the process of filing your tax returns
- Takes a reactive approach to your taxes, recording and documenting income that has already been earned, investments you already made, and expenses you already incurred
- Reduces tax liability by shifting expenses between categories

Accountants that specialize in tax preparation are unlikely to offer extensive advice on your overall tax minimization strategy. They look at your financial picture from a historical perspective, reconciling where you started with where you are now.

Any licensed CPA that has experience with tax preparation can typically handle this task, and this level of service may be right for you if your tax situation is relatively simple. For example, if all of your income is earned through your employment at a business owned by others, your tax returns should be straightforward. A tax preparer can probably meet your needs.

Taxpayers who are self-employed or own a business and those that participate in any level of investing are better off with an accountant who offers a combination of tax preparation and tax planning. This also applies to people who own real estate, because buying and selling property can carry significant tax liability if you don't plan ahead. Your Certified Tax Coach understands how to leverage tax regulations to your advantage through a comprehensive tax minimization strategy.

Tax Planning Responsibilities

- Takes a proactive approach to tax planning, looking ahead to identify opportunities for tax savings
- Advises on which assets to purchase and which investments to make in order to reduce long-term tax liability
- Reviews changes in tax law on a regular basis and ensures your strategy is adjusted accordingly over time

Accountants who want to offer tax planning services need more than the basic knowledge required for licensing exams. Adopting a proactive approach to tax planning requires a specialized skill set. Tax planners are responsible for tax preparation based on your past and present circumstances, in addition to looking ahead to create the best possible financial future.

If tax planning services are more appropriate for your situation, find an accountant who is proactive instead of reactive. One of the ways to identify a forward-thinking accountant is by asking how often you can expect to meet. Tax preparers schedule appointments once a year for the purpose of working through your return. Tax planners stay up-to-date on changes in the law and changes affecting your tax situation. They adjust your strategy year-round as your circumstances change.

You will notice that the fees charged by tax preparers are lower than those of a tax planner. It can be tempting to choose an accountant that costs less up-front. However, this plan has a significant drawback. In almost all cases, the money you save with an accountant who takes a reactive approach to your taxes doesn't make up for the extra taxes you pay when you fail to plan ahead.

Avoiding a Personality Clash

Some of the information you need to choose your accountant is available through a quick web search. For example, you can easily collect data about level of education and length of time in the field. Some firms publish websites that include additional details that may help you to understand a candidate's driving philosophies, level of risk tolerance, and other critical areas of importance.

Once you have a short list of candidates, it is time to schedule initial consultations. These meetings are your opportunity to determine whether specific accountants are a good match. You will quickly learn whether your personalities mesh, which is important in a long-term professional relationship. If you don't get along on a basic level, chances are you will have frequent, unproductive clashes.

After establishing that you will work well together, explore how the candidate approaches tax minimization. Remember, philosophies and techniques vary widely. Hiring an accountant whose perspective complements yours is a plus. Hiring one who uses tactics that make you uncomfortable simply won't work. Make sure your views are similar on tax minimization. For example, if you want to attempt every possible tax deduction, don't choose an accountant that perceives the use of tax loopholes as unethical.

Have an honest discussion about out-of-the-box thinking as it applies to deducting expenses. While you absolutely want an accountant who will ensure that you comply with the law, you may not want one who avoids all potential risks. Keep in mind that accountants face legal, financial, and professional consequences for illegal or unethical conduct, which makes some highly risk-averse.

Finally, give some thought to how you felt during the consultation. Was your opinion valued or did you feel condescended to? Did you have an opportunity to share your thoughts on tax-related topics, or was the conversation entirely one-sided? Was the appointment rushed, or did you feel valued? All of these points contribute to the likelihood of a successful working relationship. It is important to note problem areas now to prevent complications later.

Choosing the right accountant for your situation starts with a review of their education, experience, and areas of specialization. Then, make sure you are a good match when it comes to personality and financial management style. This ensures that the partnership will be successful for years to come.

Certified Tax Coaches vs. Accountants

In your search for the right accountant, you are likely to see that some of your candidates are Certified Tax Coaches. This designation distinguishes these tax planners from other professionals in the industry. Certified Tax Coaches participate in educational opportunities that are designed to increase tax planning skills. As a result, they can offer support and guidance that simply isn't available from other accountants. Some of the factors that differentiate Certified Tax Coaches include the following:

- Before they are permitted to participate in the Certified Tax Coach program, candidates must commit to a specific school of thought. Instead of operating as tax preparers, they embrace a proactive role as tax planners. These individuals are philosophically aligned with the creative thinking described in this book, and they are focused on learning how to assist clients with minimizing tax liability.

- Since Certified Tax Coaches are trained to approach tax savings proactively, they do more than simply manage the current year's tax returns. They examine your situation from a holistic perspective to design and implement a plan to reach your financial goals.

- Certified Tax Coaches approach their training with an entrepreneurial spirit, which tends to deviate from the perspective of average CPAs and accountants. Most pursue the Certified Tax Coach designation because they are excited about getting creative with tax minimization. They are enthusiastic about doing the research necessary to identify and apply lesser-known and more complex tax minimization solutions.

- The network of Certified Tax Coaches has expanded, and there are qualified professionals available nationwide. This gives you greater flexibility than you would have with a single firm or a specific accountant. You aren't tied to an individual, because you know that any Certified Tax Coach has the expertise necessary to provide high-quality tax planning services.

Trusting any professional to manage your financial affairs requires a leap of faith. Your tax filing and tax minimization strategies are critical to your long-term financial success, so this decision can have far-reaching consequences. Make sure that you don't pay unnecessary taxes by choosing the most qualified person for the job. Check for education and experience, then confirm that there is a solid match when it comes to underlying principles and philosophies.

ABOUT THE AUTHOR

Yohan J. Atlan, EA, CTC, CAA

Yohan Atlan, EA, CTC, CAA has more than 10 years of experience advising businesses and individuals on accounting and tax matters. He serves small to medium sized clients across a broad range of industries, including medical and professional practices, construction, real estate, and retail. Prior to establishing his firm, Yohan began his career with Ernst & Young, one of the Big Four accounting firms, where he performed audits of fortune 500 companies.

Yohan holds a French diplome Expert-Comptable (French CPA license), a Bachelor of Science in Accounting from Yeshiva University, and a Master of Science in Taxation from Long Island University. After earning his MS degree, he joined the LIU faculty. He is an associate tutor, teaching accounting and tax courses at the undergraduate and graduate level. Yohan is licensed as an Enrolled Agent (EA) in the United States and a Certified Accepted Agent for ITIN Application. He resides in Brooklyn, NY with his wife Sally and two sons. Yohan most enjoys spending time with his family.

Yohan J. Atlan, EA, CTC, CAA

Atlantax Group, LLC

☎ +1(212)601-2670

📍 Manhattan: 420 Lexington Avenue, Suite 1653 New York, NY 10170
Brooklyn office: 6923 8th Avenue, Brooklyn, NY 11228

🌐 www.atlantaxgroup.com

✉ yohan@atlantaxgroup.com

ACKNOWLEDGEMENTS

Writing a book is a daunting task. While it has been more rewarding than I ever considered, none of this would have been possible without our tireless Project Manager, Erikka Oxford. Erikka began her career as a part-time assistant for us while studying and putting herself through the University of California, San Diego for her degree in International Business. After graduating, she has gone on to champion books like this, ensuring that the project was organized, on time, on budget and as effective as possible. Erikka, for all this and more, thank you.

Many others have also been instrumental in bringing our message to life including Rachel Roderick, Virginia Ruehrwein, and Heidi Marttila-Losure. To all of you, a very special thank you.

Finally, to the co-authors of this book (Alexis E. Gallati, Amit Chandel, Amy Fischer, Brad Ewerth, David Auer, Dawn James, Jay Malik, Jaya R. Dahal, Kimberly C. Tara, Luke Gheen, Mike C. Manoloff, Peter Freuler, Randy Jenkins, Sandy Suchoff, Tina Pittman, William Stukey, and Yohan Atlan), your desire and willingness to provide this message to everyday business owners is so appreciated. While many of America's most profitable companies pay very little in tax, it is the masses of every day ordinary businesses who make our country successful. Thank you for bringing your expertise to enable them to put more money into what they love.

APPENDIX

The Tax Cuts and Jobs Act Overview

On December 22, 2017, the largest tax reform in three decades, the Tax Cuts and Jobs Act, was passed. The article is dedicated to providing some guidance on the tax reform and aid in preparing for planning. The reform impacts individual and business taxes in 2017 and beyond. While much of the impact will be seen in 2018 through 2025, the changes could revert back to its current state if the future Congress does not extend the Act. That means that the individual tax changes would reset, and the tax law would return to the 2017 state that we all know of today.

For tax years 2018 through 2025, the changes present a number of year-end tax planning opportunities.

Individual Tax Implications

Income Tax Rate		Income Levels for Those Filing As:	
2017	2018-2025	Single	Married-Joint
10%	10%	$0-$9,525	$0-$19,050
15%	12%	$9,525-$38,700	$19,050-$77,400
25%	22%	$38,700-$82,500	$77,400-$165,000
28%	24%	$82,500-$157,500	$165,000-$315,000
33%	32%	$157,500-$200,000	$315,000-$400,000
33%-35%	35%	$200,000-$500,000	$400,000-$600,000
39.6%	37%	$500,000+	$600,000+

Standard deduction – The Act increases the standard deduction through 2025.
- Single Filers – $6,500 to $12,000
- Married filing jointly – $13,000 to $24,000
- Heads of households – $9,500 to $18,000

Affordable Care Act – aka "Obamacare" – Repeals the penalty imposed on those who do not obtain insurance in 2019.

Personal Exemptions – Repeals all personal exemptions through 2025.

Itemized Deductions – The Act eliminates or restricts the ability to use several itemized deductions, through 2025.

State and Local Taxes OR Property Tax Deductions – Individuals are allowed a maximum deduction and must choose between state and local income or property taxes.
- Married filing jointly – $10,000
- Married filing separately – $5,000

Mortgage Interest – Limits the debt of the loan by filing status. Mortgages taken out or contracts entered into before Dec. 15, 2017, are still subject to the current tax laws.
- Married filing jointly – first $750,000

Home Equity Loans – Repealed through 2025.

Alternative Minimum Tax (AMT) – Raises the exemption amount and exemption phaseout threshold that was enacted to curb tax avoidance **among high earners**.
- **Married couples filing jointly** – Exemption increases to $109,400 and phaseout increases to $1,000,000.
- **All other taxpayers** – Exemption increases to $70,300 and phaseout increases to $500,000 (other than estates and trusts).

Casualty Losses – Applies only if the loss is attributable to a presidentially declared disaster.

Gambling Losses – The bill clarifies that the term "losses from wagering transactions" in Sec. 165(d) includes any otherwise allowable deduction incurred in carrying on a wagering transaction. This is intended to clarify that the limitation of losses from wagering transactions applies not only to the actual costs of wagers, but also to other expenses incurred by the taxpayer in connection with his or her gambling activity.

Charitable Contributions – The charitable contributions changes are limited or repealed.

- Increases the income-based percentage limit for charitable contributions of cash to public charities to 60%.
- Donations given in exchange for college seating tickets or athletics events are no longer allowed.

Miscellaneous Itemized Deductions – All miscellaneous itemized deductions subject to the 2% floor under current law are repealed through 2025.

Medical Expenses – Allows for medical expense deductions in excess of 10% of adjusted gross income.

Child Tax Credit – The Act has several tax planning advantages.

- Increases the Child Tax Credit from $1,000 to $2,000 per child.
- The credit is refundable for qualifying taxpayers up to $1,400.
- Increases the maximum income level to qualify for the credit.
  - $400,000 for married taxpayers filing a joint return.
  - $200,000 for other taxpayers.
- Expansion of 529 savings plans.
  - Maximum distribution of $10,000 per student for tuition at private and religious K-12 schools.
  - Allows parents to use the funds for expenses for home-schooled students.

IRA Recharacterizations – The Act repeals the ability to recharacterize one kind of IRA contribution as another, for example to designate a traditional contribution as a Roth contribution, or vice-versa.

Estate, Gift, and Generation-Skipping Transfer Taxes – This change will be reversed as of 2026.

The estate tax doubles the exemption and applies to estates of decedents dying and gifts made after Dec. 31, 2017, and before Jan. 1, 2026.

- $11.2 million for singles
- $22.4 million for couples

Other Credits – The Act repeals several tax credits.

- Credit for the elderly and permanently disabled.
- Credit for plug-in electric drive motor vehicles.
- Credit for interest on certain home mortgages.

Other Deduction Changes – The Act outlines other impacts to the individual taxpayer.

- **Alimony** – Alimony and separate maintenance payments are not deductible by the payor spouse and conversely not includible income by the payee spouse.
- **Moving Expenses** – Repealed for most with one major exception.
  - Members of the armed forces on active duty who move because of military orders or a change in where the members is stationed.
- **Exclusion for Bicycle Commuting Reimbursements** – The bill repeals through 2025 the exclusion from gross income or wages of qualified bicycle commuting expenses.

Business Tax Implications

For tax years beginning after Dec. 31, 2017, and beginning before Jan. 1, 2026, the Tax Reform and Jobs Act include the following changes that impact businesses.

Alternative Minimum Tax (AMT): Eliminated for corporations.

Income from Pass-Through Entities: The Act dramatically changes how individuals are taxed on income from partnerships, S corporations, and other pass-through entities.

- Increases deductions to 20% of "qualified business income" from a partnership, S corporation, or sole proprietorship.
  - "Qualified business income" means the net amount of qualified items of income, gain, deduction, and loss with respect to the qualified trade or business of the taxpayer.
  - Items must be conducted trade or business within the United States. They do not include specified investment-related income, deductions, or losses.
  - "Qualified business income" does not include an S corporation shareholder's reasonable compensation, guaranteed payments, or—to the extent provided in regulations—payments to a partner who is acting in a capacity other than his or her capacity as a partner.
  - "Specified service trades or businesses" include any trade or business in the fields of accounting, health, law, consulting, athletics, financial services, brokerage services, or any business where the principal asset of the business is the reputation or skill of one or more of its employees.
  - The exclusion from the definition of a qualified business for specified service trades or businesses phases in for a taxpayer with taxable income:
    - Singles – $157,500
    - Married filing jointly – $315,000

- Allowed deductions of 20% of qualified real estate investment trust (REIT) dividends, qualified cooperative dividends, and qualified publicly traded partnership income. (Special rules apply to specified agricultural or horticultural cooperatives.)
- Limitation on deduction based on W-2 wages above a threshold amount of taxable income, generally limited to 50%.
- Deduction disallows for specified service trades or businesses with income above a threshold.
- For each qualified trade or business, can deduct 20% of the qualified business income with respect to such trade or business.
- Capital-intensive businesses may yield a higher benefit under a rule that takes into consideration 25% of wages paid plus a portion of the business's basis in its tangible assets.

Corporate Income Tax Rate Reduction: The Act reduces the corporate income tax rate and expands property definitions.

- Reduces tax rate beginning in 2018 to 21 percent from 35 percent.
- Allows 100 percent expensing for business property placed in service after September 27, 2017 to encourage more capital investing in corporations
- Expands eligible property definition for 100 percent expensing, to include used property that was not previously used by the taxpayer. Expires in 2023 or 2024 for certain property.

International Tax Reform: The Act makes significant changes to the U.S. international tax code.

- Entirely replaces the current foreign subsidiaries system with a dividend exemption system. U.S. corporations are exempt from U.S. income tax for foreign-source dividends and certain foreign subsidiaries are exempt from U.S. income tax.
- Requires foreign subsidiaries to pay a repatriation tax on their foreign subsidiaries' post-1986 earnings and profits.

- Tax is 14.5 percent on foreign earnings held in cash and cash equivalents.

- 7.5 percent on foreign earnings held in illiquid assets.

- Imposes current U.S. income tax on 50 percent of foreign controlled corporation. Under the system, multinationals are taxed on foreign earned income.

Carried Interest: The Act addresses the tax of "carried interest," directed at private equity fund managers, hedge fund managers, and some other investment professionals to pay long-term capital gains rates on their share of the profits from an investment partnership.

- Beginning 2019, long-term capital gains attributable to an "applicable partnership interest" are characterized as short-term capital gain (taxable at ordinary income rates) to the extent applicable to an investment held less than three years.

- An applicable partnership interest generally means a partnership interest transferred about the performance of substantial services. In effect, the provision does not allow fund managers to benefit from the lower tax rate applicable to long-term capital gains unless the investment that generated the gain was held for at least three years.

Liquor Tax: The Act cuts taxes on beer, wine, and liquor.

One thing is clear: The tax reform plan will mean different things to different people, depending on how much they make, where they live, and their family size and makeup. See your tax planning professional for the best tax implementation plan for you, your family, and your business. The implications could have both negative and positive effects, so get the facts for your circumstances and ensure you escape the tax increase!